©copyright of artist Kofi Boamah

P**K II

Kofi N.Boamah

a peintturé in words

entiendo's

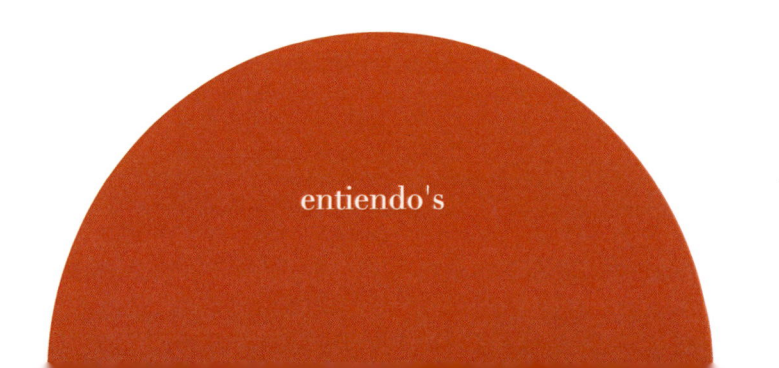

...There is a close relantionship between flowers & convicts...**Our Lady of Flowers, JEAN GENET...**

PURETABOO...

BenWay's GP 65 Dalston Lane
London E8 2NG

...waking up with 'sweatitty' & a humongous 'period' pan au chocolairy feeling in the her 'camel toe' area...the Pharmacy I'd advise...

...Lemsip for any Cold Sore Symptoms
...Pepto Bismal (for the Pan Au Chocolairy 'issue') Vitamin B & C...
...juice & plenty of Vegetables...
...& DO feed THI$ Cat, Chancie...

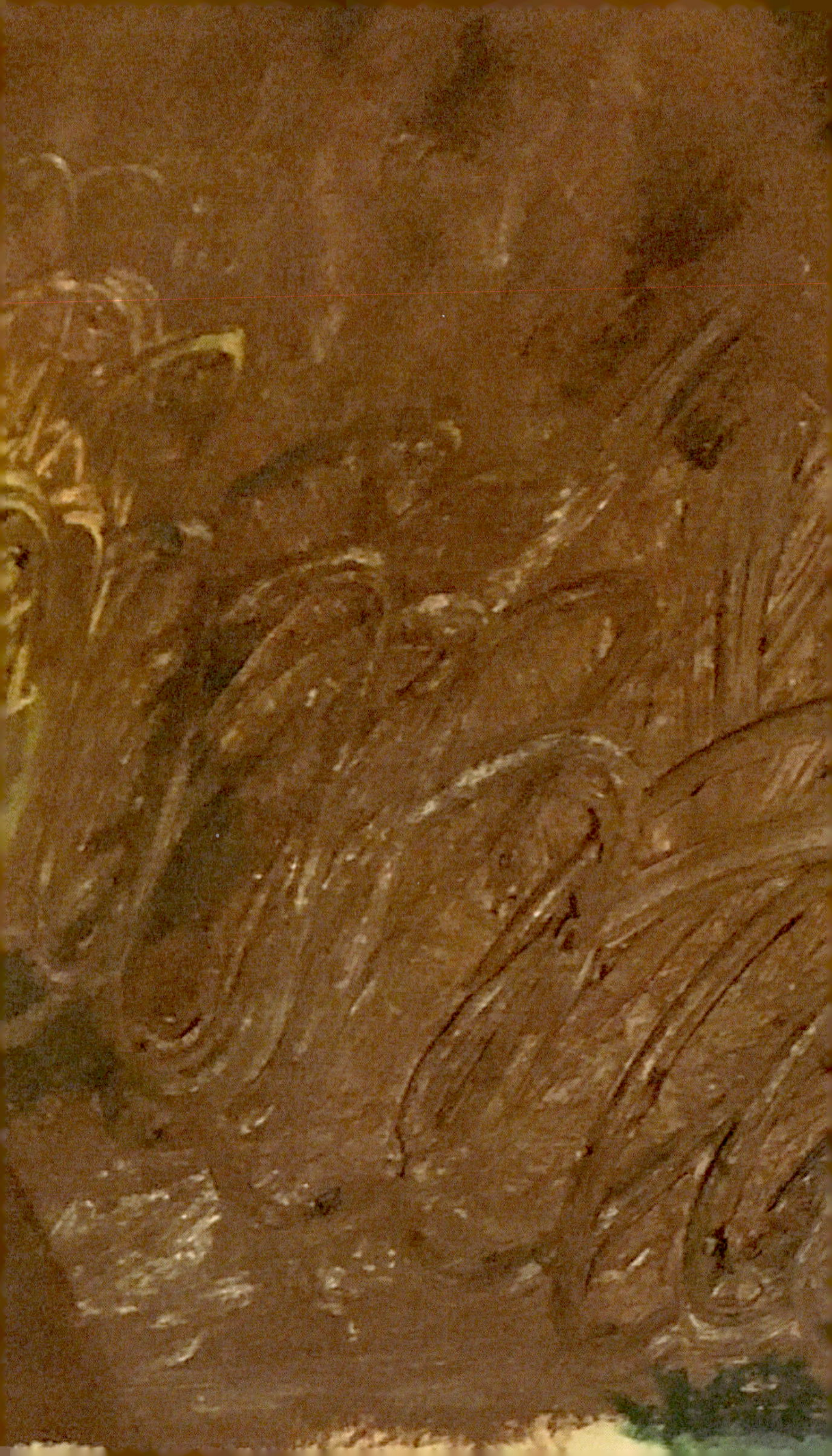

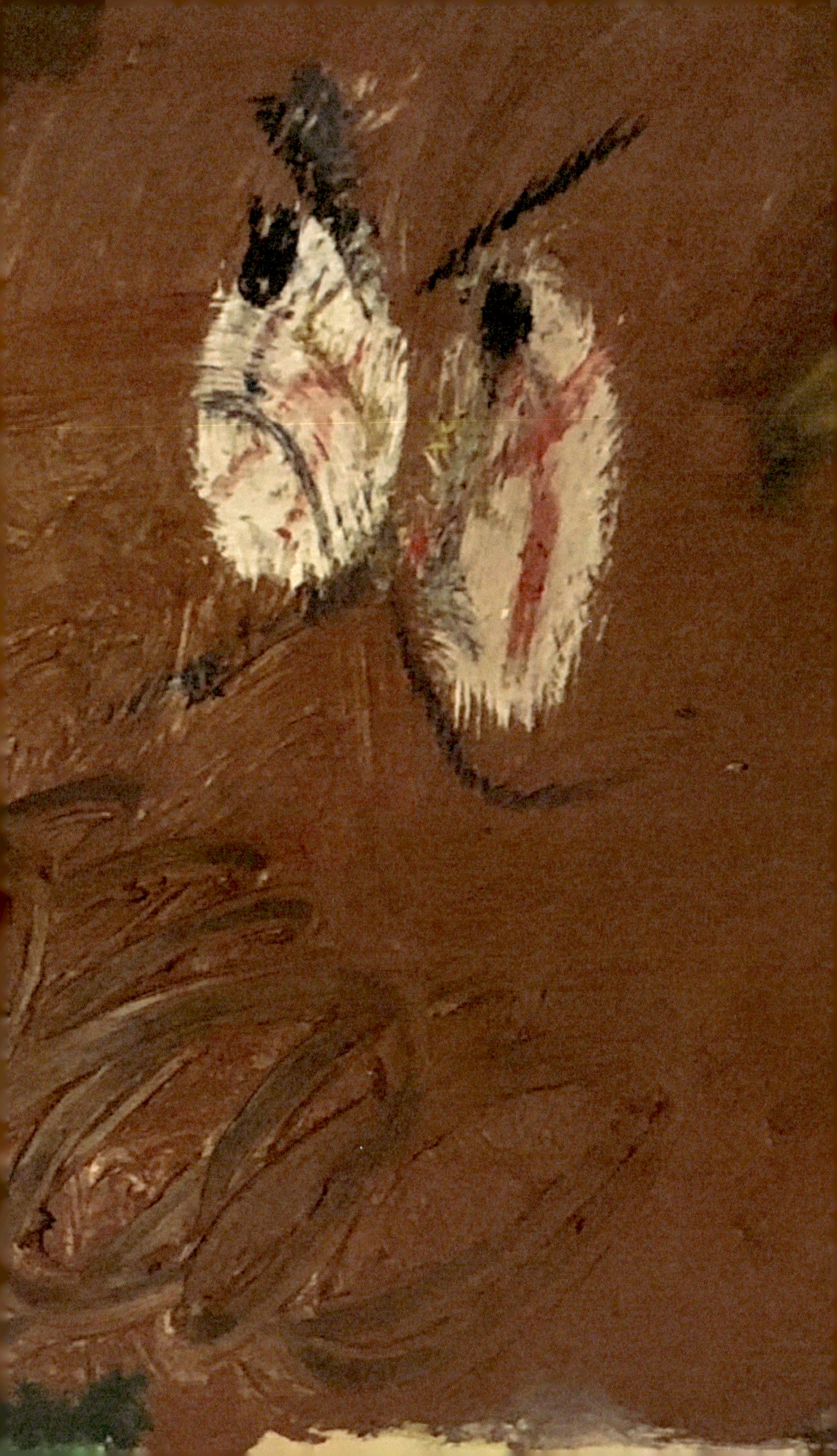

priapristic dollop$

BenWay's GP 65 Dalston Lane
London E8 2NG

...he came back two months after complaining of gout on his foot...prescribing a balm or 'Maggi' for this...also try & go for walks more...than four Days a week...

*Lemsip
Vitamin D...

65 Dalston Lane
London E8 2NG
United Kingdom

...smelling of Roses & whispering about 'a Man**'
I'd advise carrying on there...however try these
condoms as your Period Pain...being that it's
late...& you have á *HEAVY FLOW* ..:Tampons will
help this but we may need another *'Gynecology'*
appointment...ask Kat to also get you Condoms...

x 14 Nurofen (Cum back in a month)
headache capsules (Newton'$)

..:

BenWay's GP 65 Dalston Lane
London E8 2NG

not seen her in a while...the sunshine seems gone...as AI but without the green shards of breeze she sings a melody even the moments of labia against HAND$...Kat advises you not to speak of Poetry...as clearly THE NEW JOB is too strenuous...advise to keep going...break a leg...

Marijuana (to help sleep)
fruit & vegetables
Pepto Bismal x 28
 Vitmin C & L...

BenWay's GP 65 Dalston Lane
London E8 2NG

...seem to arrive two weeks after í booked You in for an appointment...try, along with this PRESCRIPTION, MARCUS OIL...& below too...

Pepto Bismal
Vix (any brand) for you're FOOT
with only two capsules of Lemsip & the sniff
here...sack it off &

suck it up...ok
3x Vitamin D (FUMIN' Brand)

BenWay's GP 65 Dalston Lane
London E8 2NG
United Kingdom

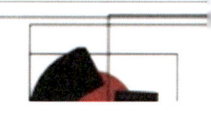

…'it's all too much they're out to keeeeeeIII' y0U don't worry here…take this Lemsip & tell your Wife Chancie is MISSING !!! & Open both your EYES when 'it's all too much, no..? a bit like your friend Mabankou…'

1x Lemsip
Castor oils
Cod Liver Oil
2x EYE DROPS
1x Vitamin D

BenWay's GP 65 Dalston Lane
London E8 2NG
United Kingdom

...dropping in at half past three (for your appoinment) 'swearing of raging' PERIOD PAIN ! & an emergenCy on a BlKE...thos PESKY BlKES...advise...vegetables & fruits...

144x Lemsip Capsules
Rosewater
& another appointment TOMORROW TOMORROW, TOMORROW...

DR.DAN...

BenWay's GP
65 Dalston Lane
London E8 2NG
United Kingdom

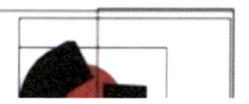

...Dr. Dan (a fellow Gynecologist & Partner) advising these walk$...
...
...
...(redacted in a COURT of LAW)
...
...
28x Lemsip
Rosewater
Pepto Bismal for the awful period cramps...they're 'ooouuufff the Richter' she says...which Richter she mentions *OF* is beyond...it's a drop of heaven seeing her swaying hips move in & out...ín & out...& ín with a need for more & never any possibility of any more...[addicted]...

Pascal
Wa

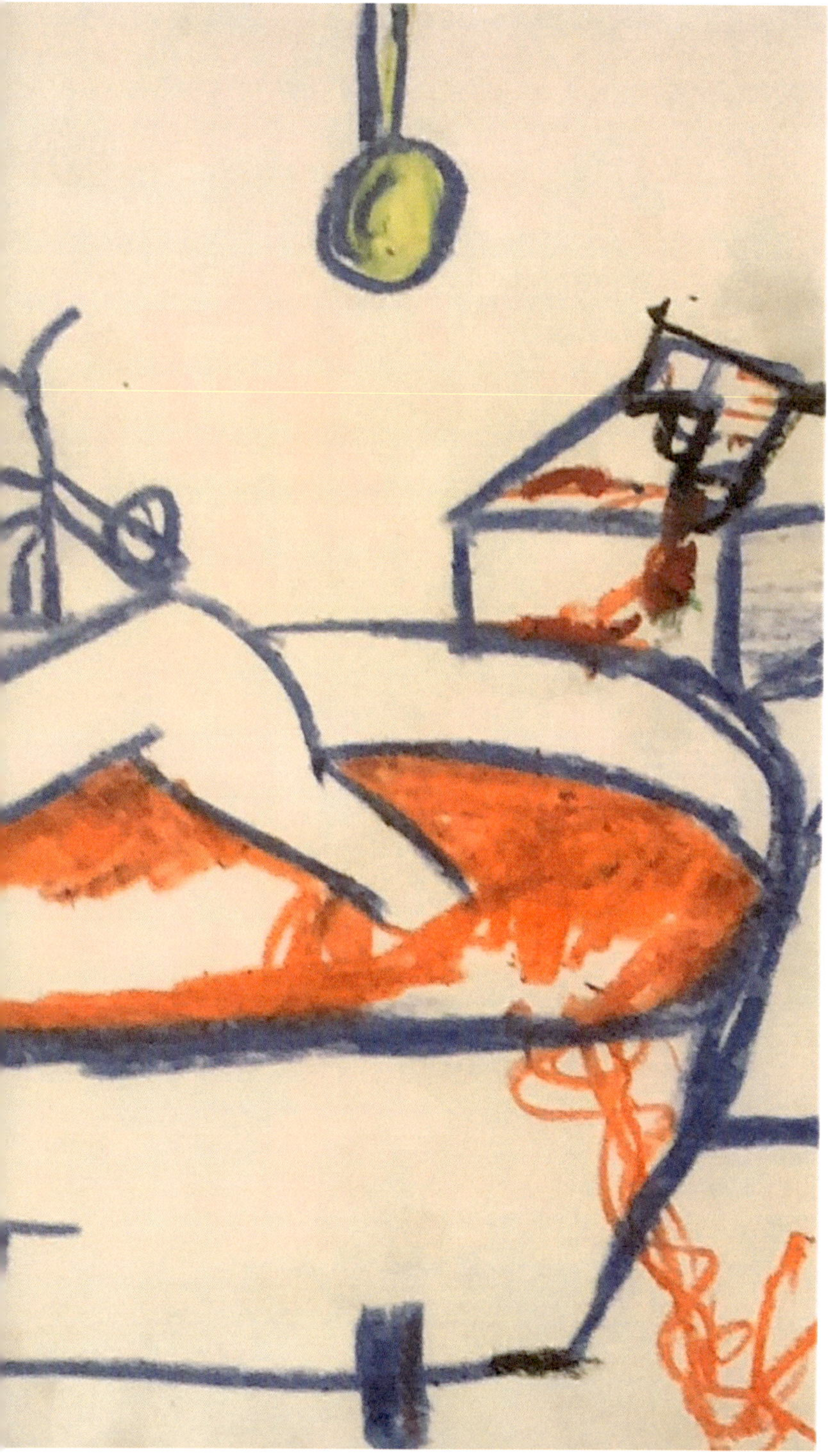

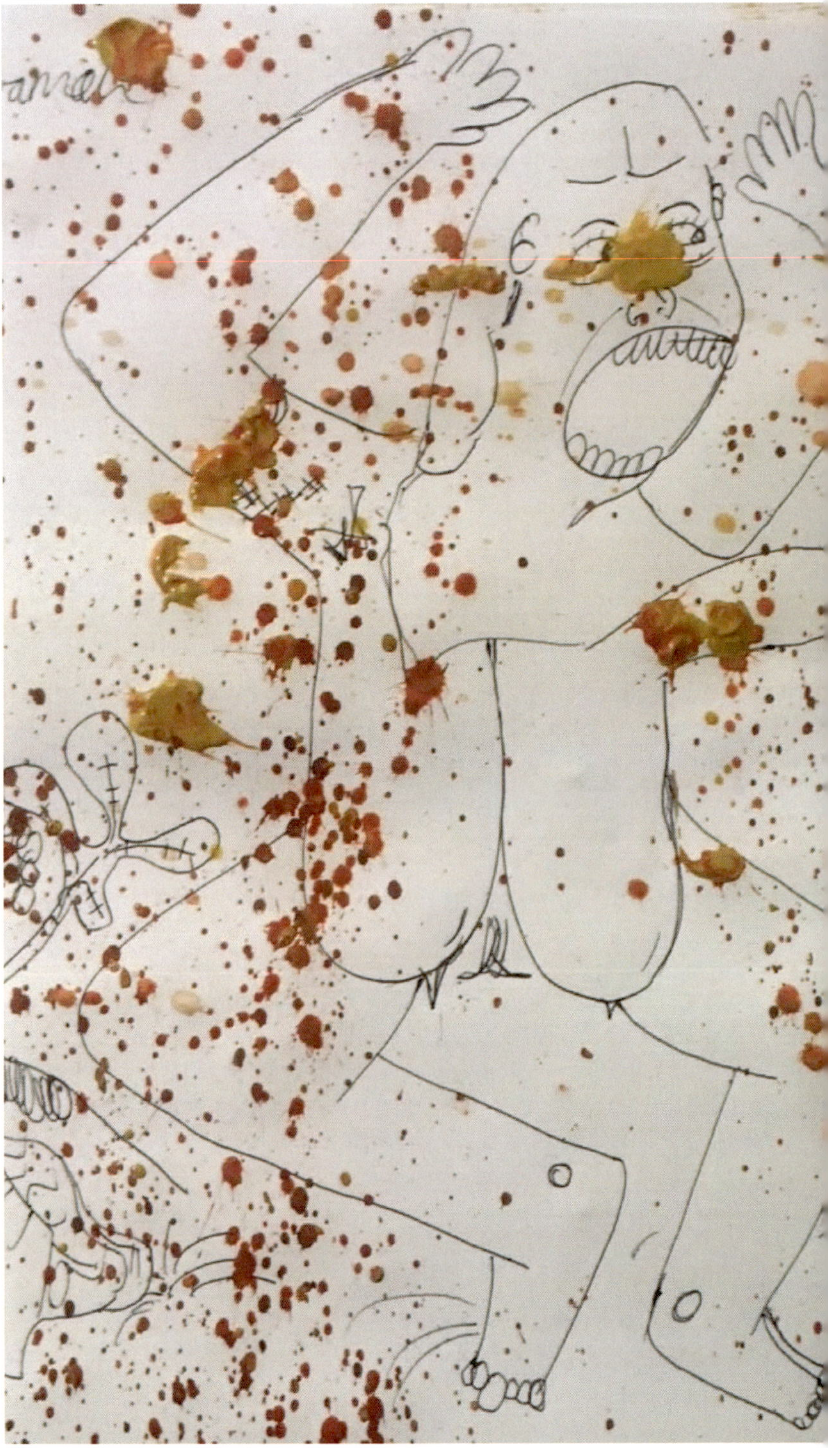

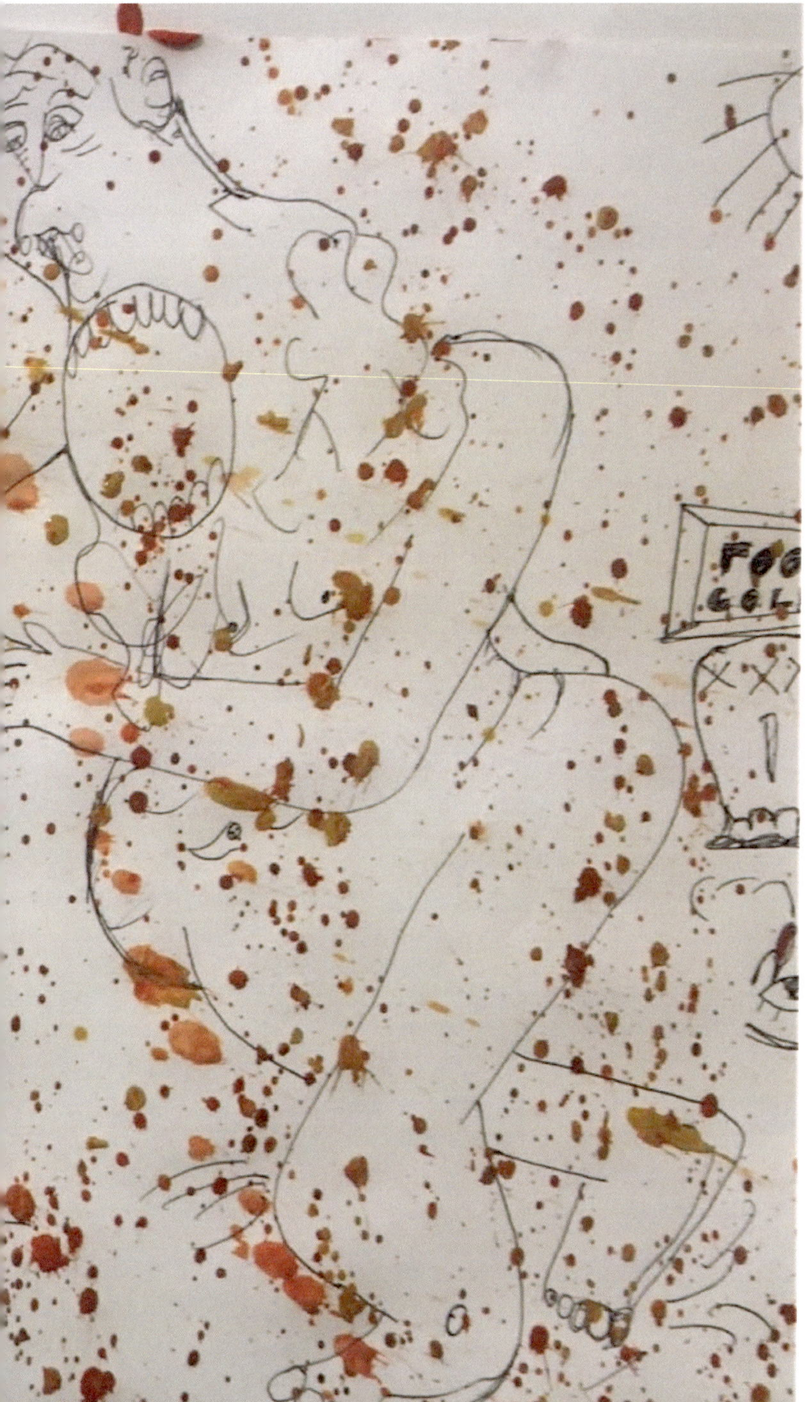

BenWay's GP

65 Dalston Lane
London E8 2NG

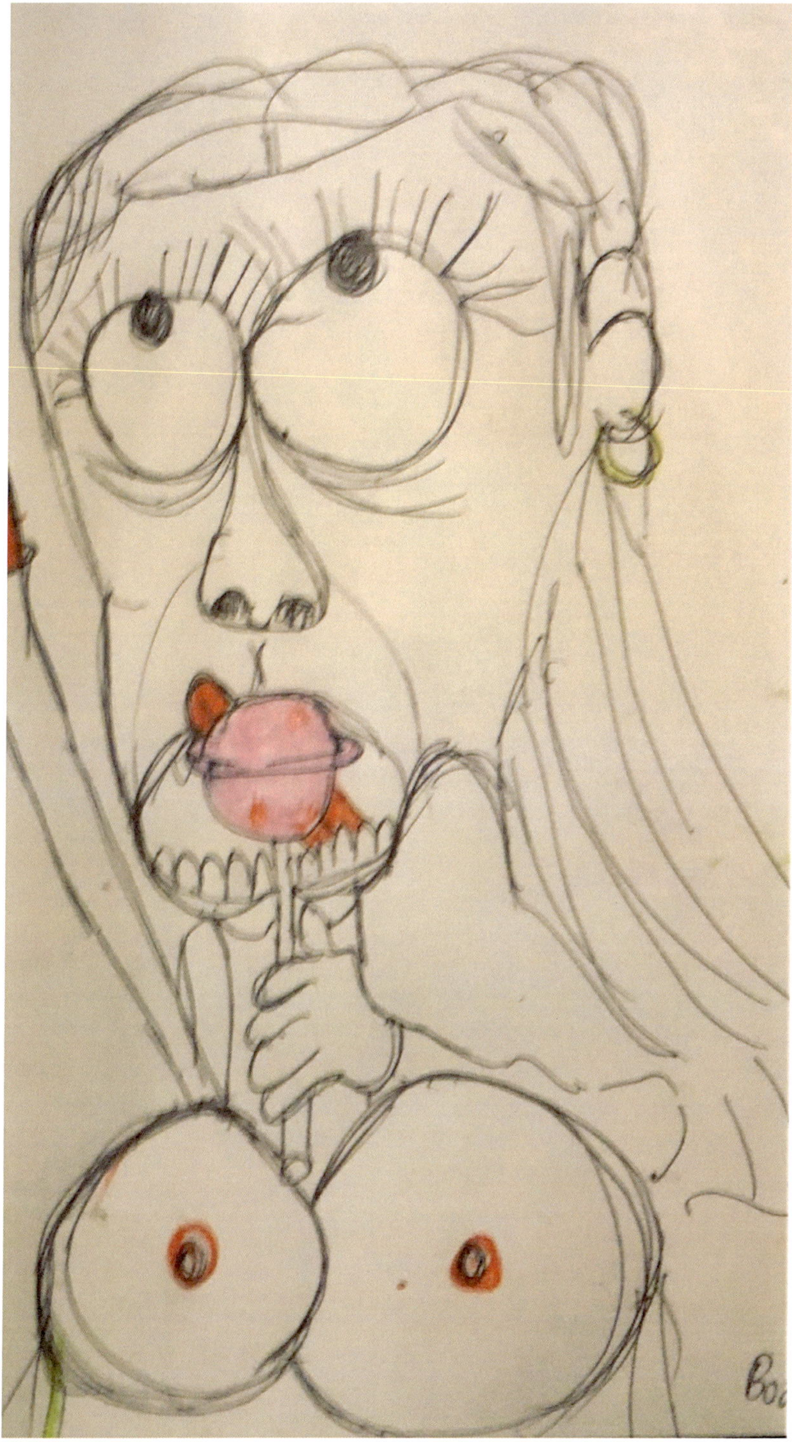

CRO$$ THAT LIN$...
CRO$$ THAT LIN$...
CRO$$ THAT LIN$...

BenWay's GP 65 Dalston Lane
London E8 2NG
United Kingdom

...arriving 'Hot Eared' & shouting at Kat (excessively loudly)...'advise'

±auce (a brand this will keep you hush hush HU$*)
14 x Lemsip (just two *weak's of dosess...* as it's nearly Summer again)

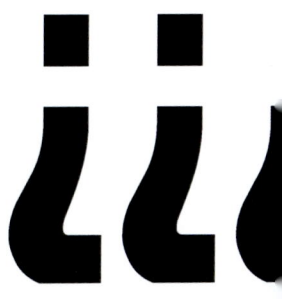

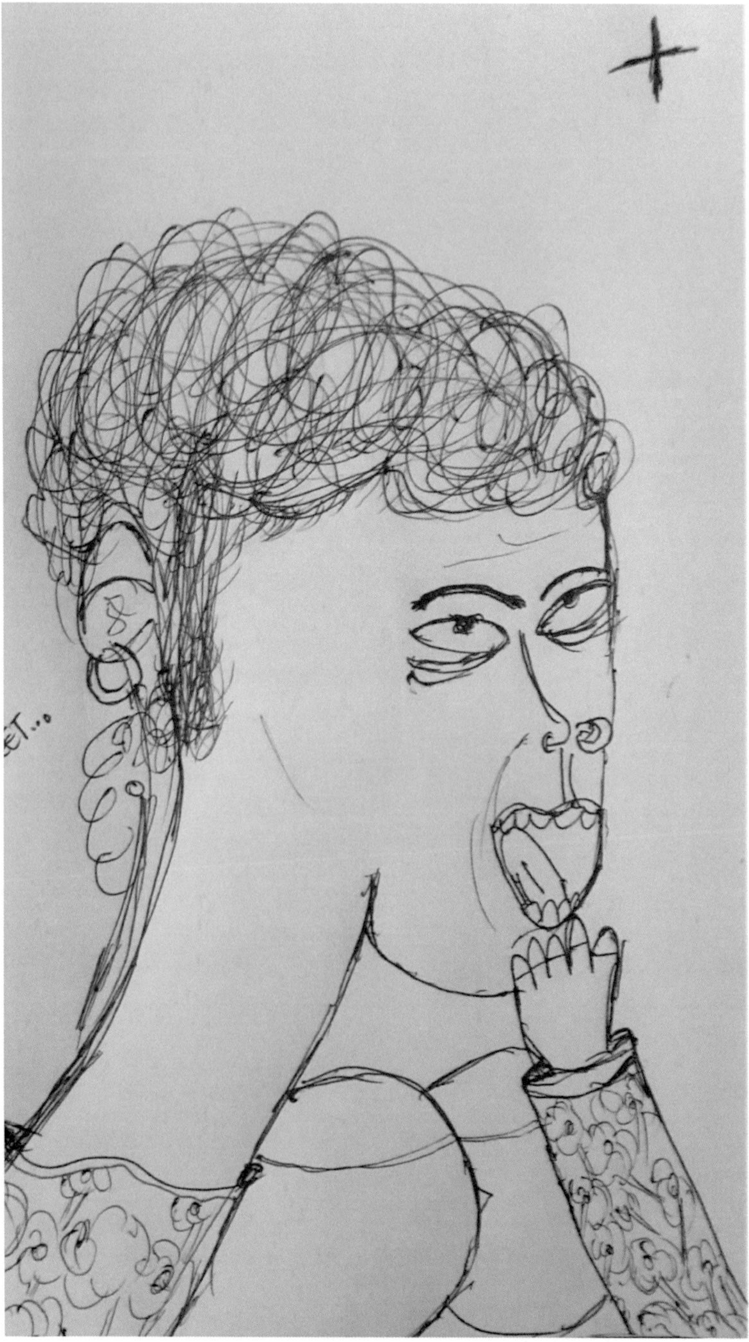

BenWay's GP

65 Dalston Lane
London E8 2NG

BenWay's GP 65 Dalston Lane
London E8 2NG

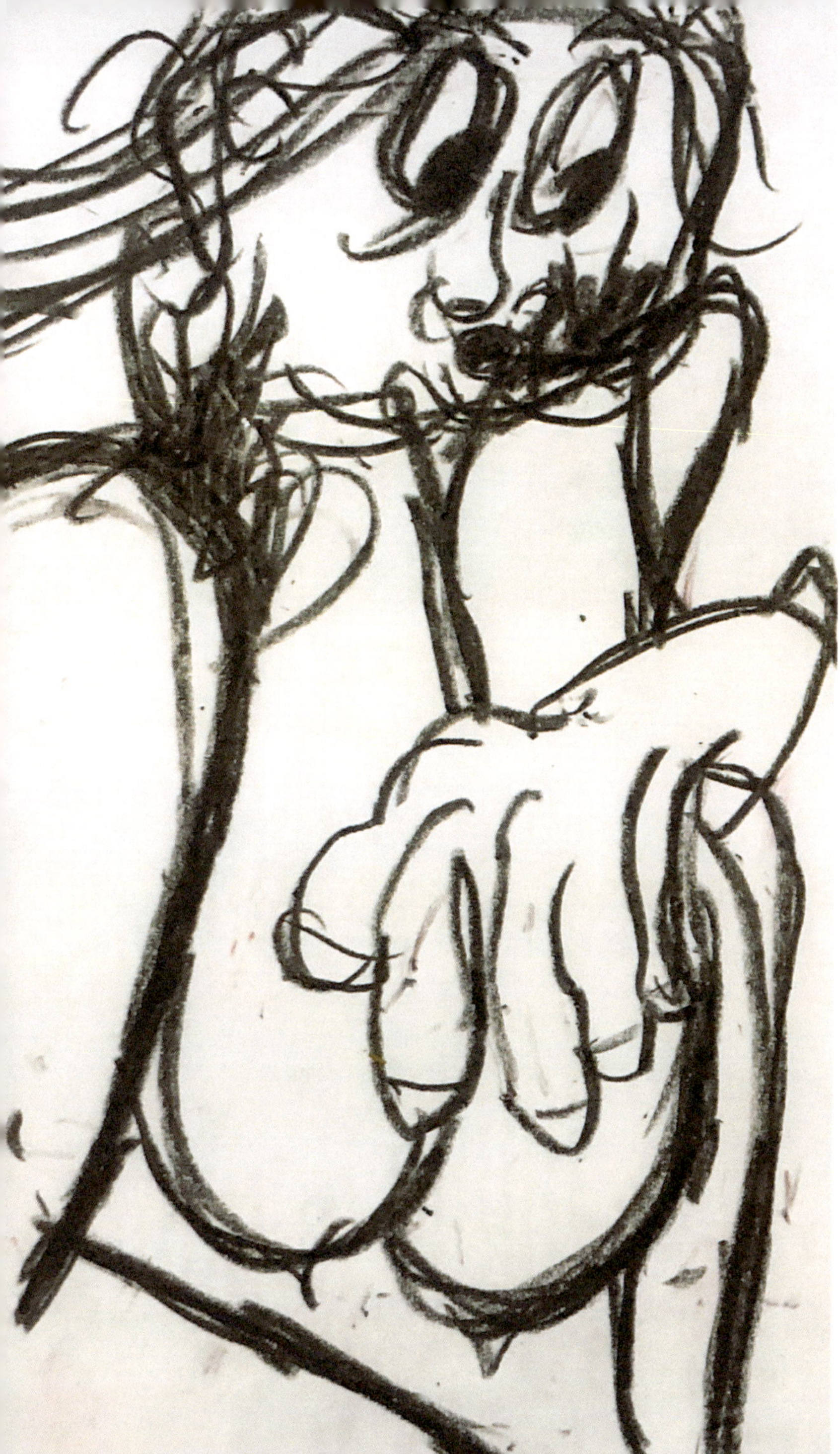

BenWay's GP 65 Dalston
London E8

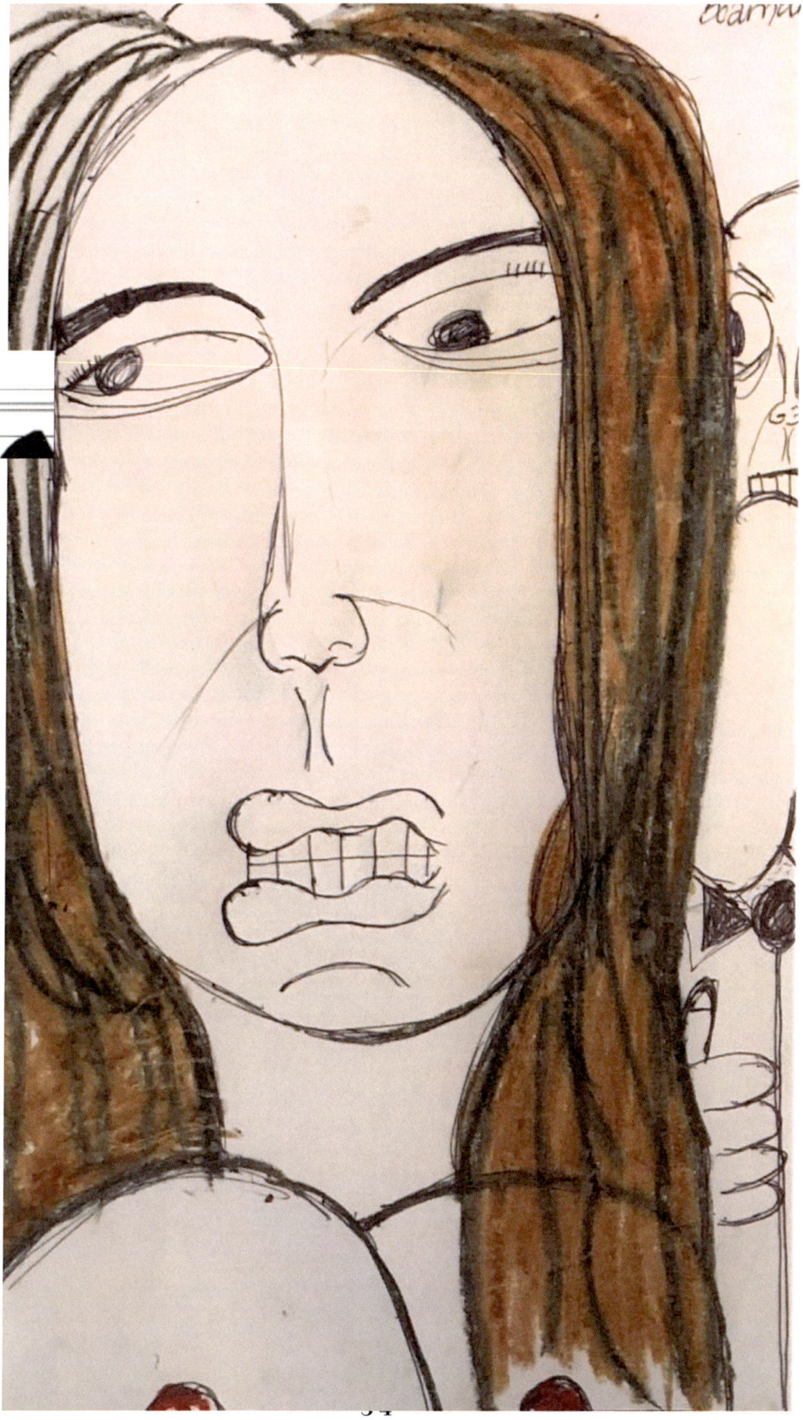

BenWay's GP

65 Dalston Lane
London E8 2NG

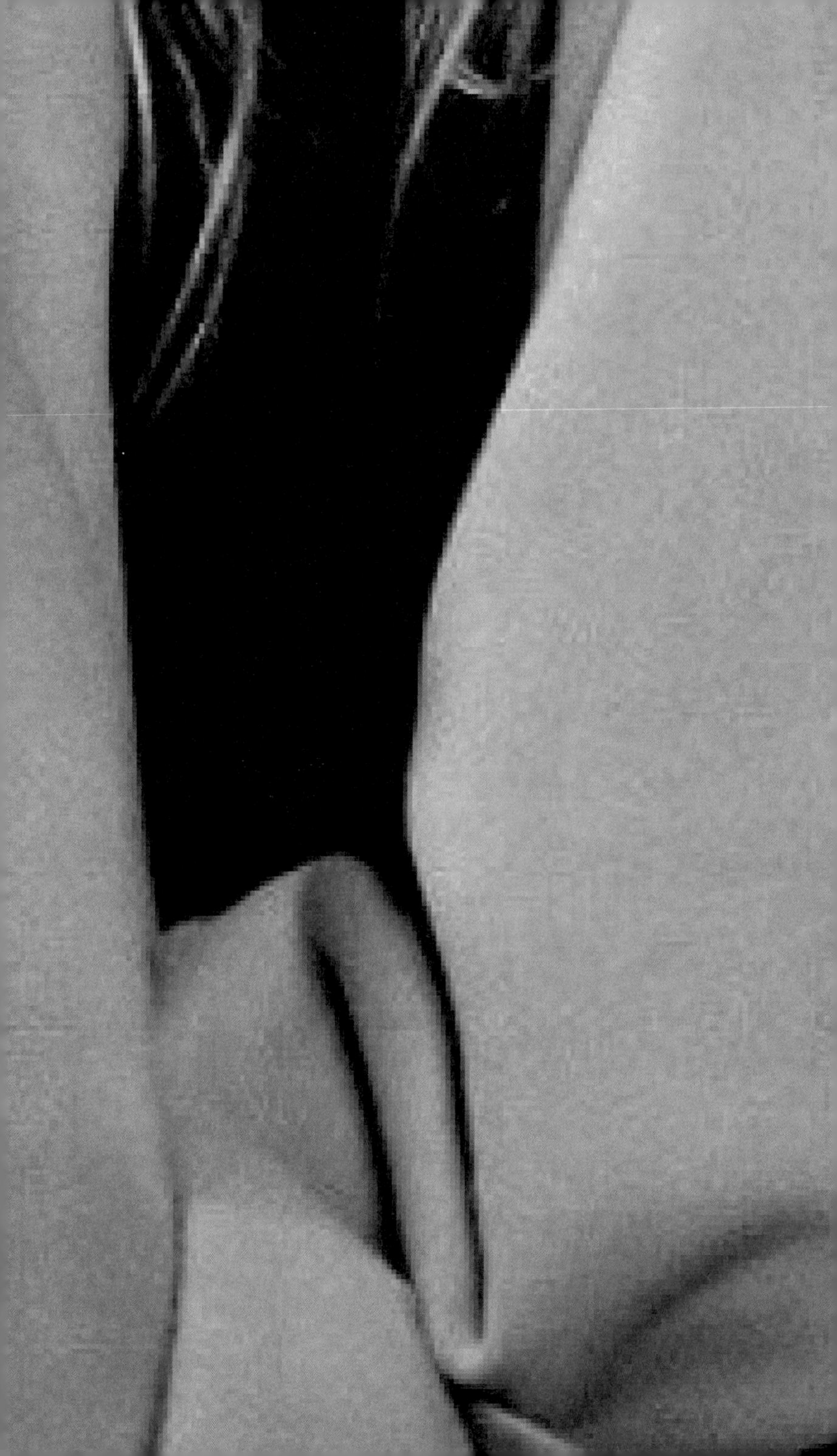

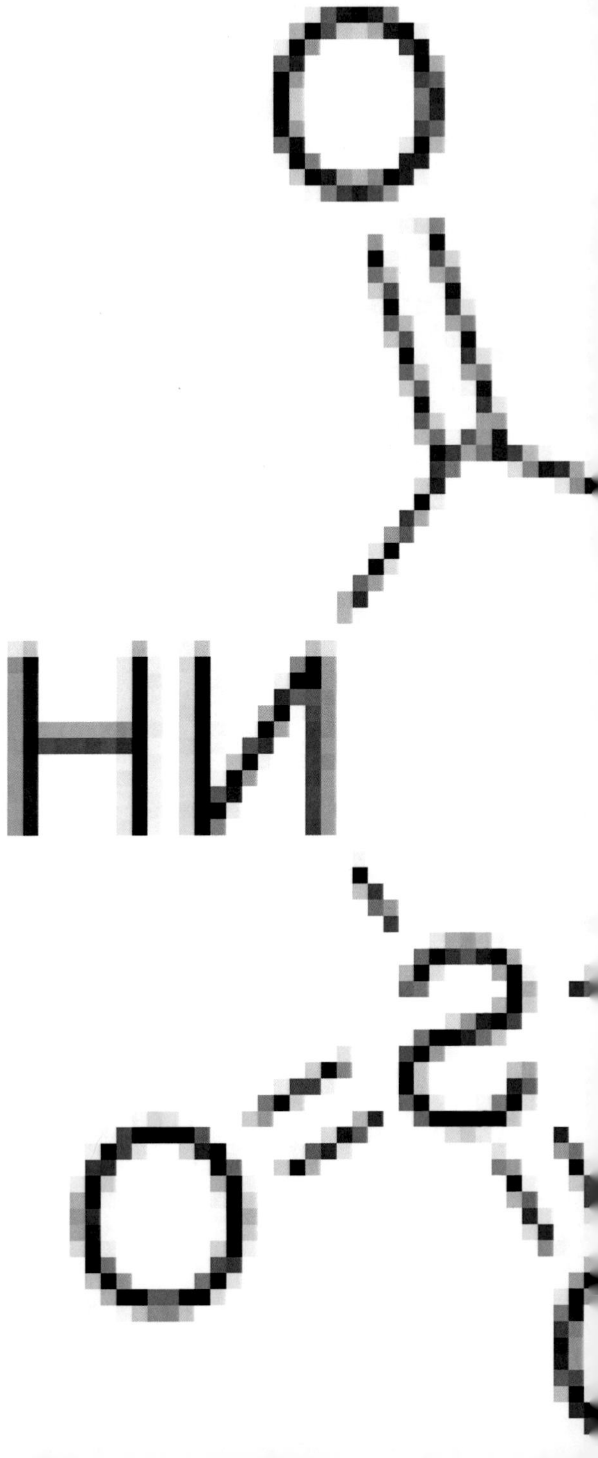

BenWay's GP

65 Dalston Lane
London E8 2NG

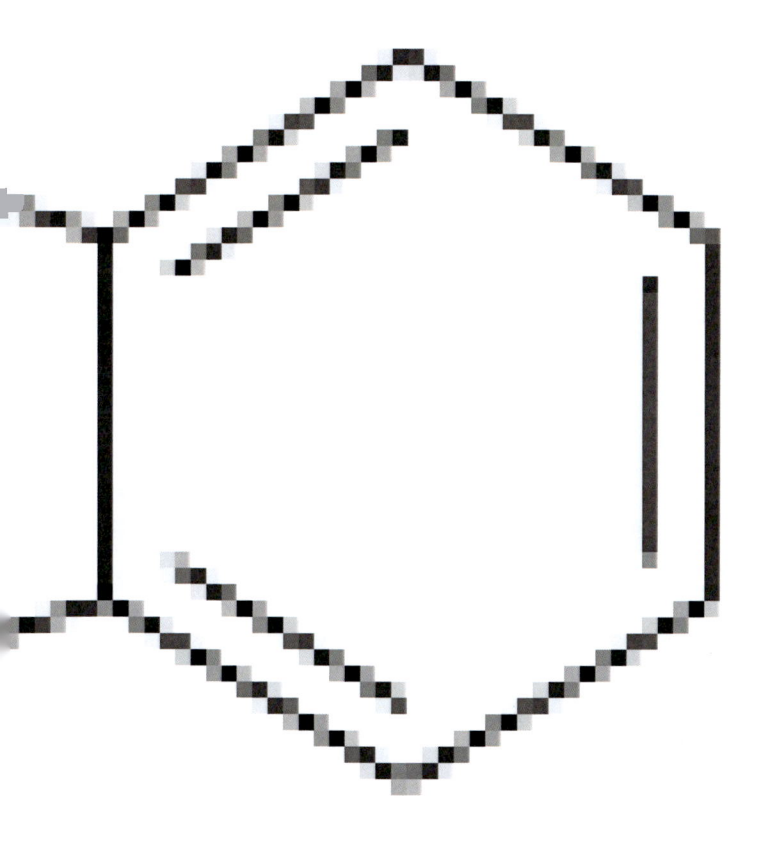

...nothin

prescrib

...nothing to

...nothing to *

"Ananda Santo.

g to
e...

BenWay's GP 65 Dalston Lane
London E8 2NG

HERE LISSON
@STONERTKM

prescribe...

escribe...

"",,,

,,,

....

thigh

s

DDDDDD

¿ ¨ ,,, ,,,

uice on her

.i prescribe

me Vitamin

ODD...

,,,

chubbyback...
GLASGOW NIGHT$...

65 Dalston Lane
London E8 2NG

big

white

period

Panties...

.....

...BURGUNDY DRIPS
...DRIPS
...DRIPS
KAZ' DRIPS
...Drip...

*SOCRATES' WARNING GOD of
the whiskeys..*

...SOCRATE$ 'SEVENTY ONE ROSES...

DRIP AGAINST THE FIG GET THE MONEY LEAVES KETCHUPING WITH TOO MUCH SAUCE ON HIS CHIPS...

SOCRATE$ SEVENTY ONE ROSES...

WILL IS THAT YOOOOOOOOOOOOOOOUUUUU...

MARCUS IS THAT YOOOOOOOOOOOOOOOOOUU...

KWABS IS THAT YOU$$$$$$$$

BenWay's GP
65 Dalston Lane
London E8 2NG

DRIP AGAINST THE FIG GET THE MONEY LEAVES KETCHUPING WITH TOO MUCH SAUCE ON HIS CHIPS...

SOCRATE$ SEVENTY ONE ROSES...

WILL IS THAT YOOOOOOOOOOOOOOOUUUUU...

MARCUS IS THAT YOOOOOOOOOOOOOOOOOUU...

KWABS IS THAT YOU$$$$$$$$

BenWay's

65 Dalston Lane
London E8 2NG

BenWay

GANT GANTRY TO

65 Dalston Lane
London E8 2NG

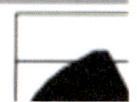

ER HEART...

BenWay's GP

65 Dalston Lane
London E8 2NG

BenWay's GP

Dalston Lane
London E8 2NG

BenWay's GP

65 Dalston Lane
London E8 2NG

BenWay's GP

65 Dalston Lane
London E8 2NG

BenWay's GP

65 Dalston Lane
London E8 2NG

~~Dr Benway~~

65 Dalston Lane
London E8 2NG
United Kingdom

...as you've not been sick for at least eight months...'medical marijuana' seems appropriate...
5x Vix Palm (brand Viera)
x 3 Lemsip
x 2 Cod Liver Oil
salt (an old therapy for that wound, so ask Kat for 'a Dollop' the pharmacy can provide)
OJ

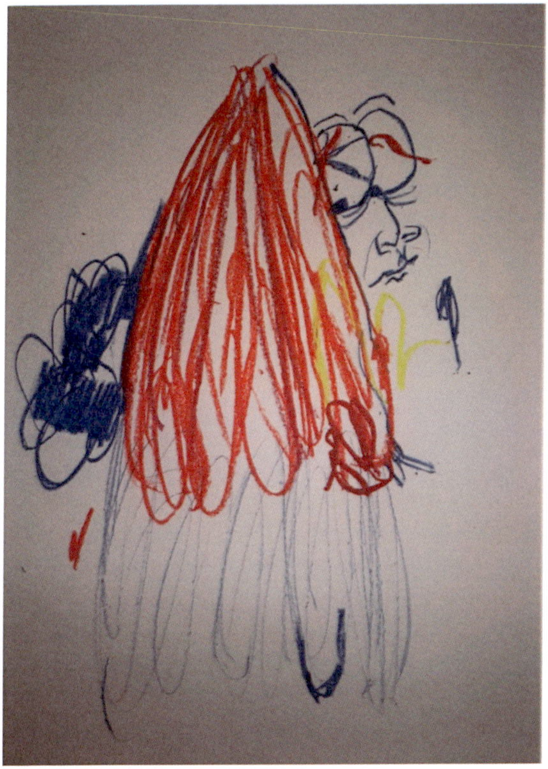

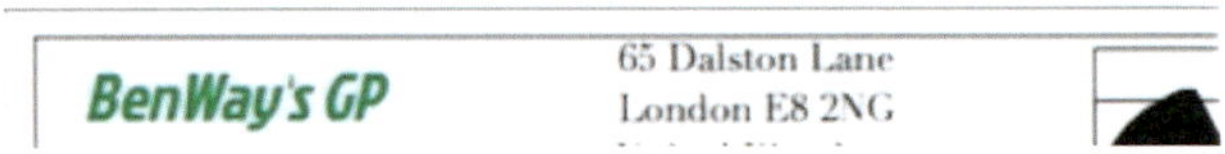
BenWay's GP
65 Dalston Lane
London E8 2NG

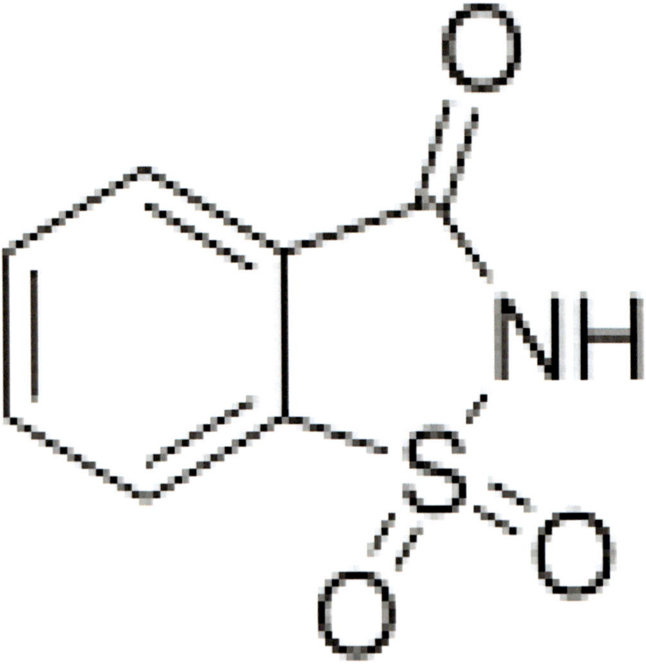

~~Dr Benway~~ 65 Dalston Lane
London E8 2NG
United Kingdom

...it's been months since she cum...& so arriving with the meds
bottle I gave her...it's all 'tippy' again down below...I say...do you
swallow...swallow...swallow...i prescribed Mayonaise & told her that
he probably be the last to know about all this 'Mayonaise' spillage
& it's just spillage...it's not on that I can get accused by Mrs Corona
for apparently...'butchering Kat, albeit CONSENTUALLY !!!
Nurofin...& Milk............t i   t t
SY...

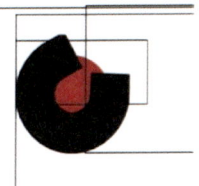

BenWay's GP   65 Dalston Lane
London E8 2NG
United Kingdom

...'it's all ooouuueeef' nothin' is True he is saying...whilst screaming...i put the vanilla ice cream down & told him...it's ooonnn...i stood from behind the desk to reinforce this...Pepo Bismal should clear this right up & spot of a few condoms & *mango* flavoured lube because she loves *mango*...

BenWay's GP
65 Dalston Lane
London E8 2NG
United Kingdom

...'apparently' a tippy Pain on the left of Vaginé has led
advising 'a quickie' which enabled 'a relief' which she
made her feel brand new & a bit like how Nkuk 'makes' her
feel...after a flood of tears...& a slap against her wet *labia*...she
felt less disheartened...Lemsip three times a week & make an
appointment with Kat...the administrator...

BenWay's GP   65 Dalston Lane
London E8 2NG
United Kingdom

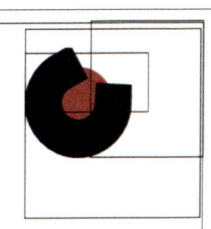

Patient seems 'Soupy'
I've advised Strawberry Lemsip, which is given in caps & able to gain purchase of due to an Anxiety with Wife (whom he deems 'ball & chain') two scoops of butters I said in the Morning will help with that & is exactly what the Doctors advises...Medical 'Green' seems appropriate too...maybe a capsule of Valium for 'right eye ticky sleeping' problem...I prognosed too slaps on bottom...

Dr Benway

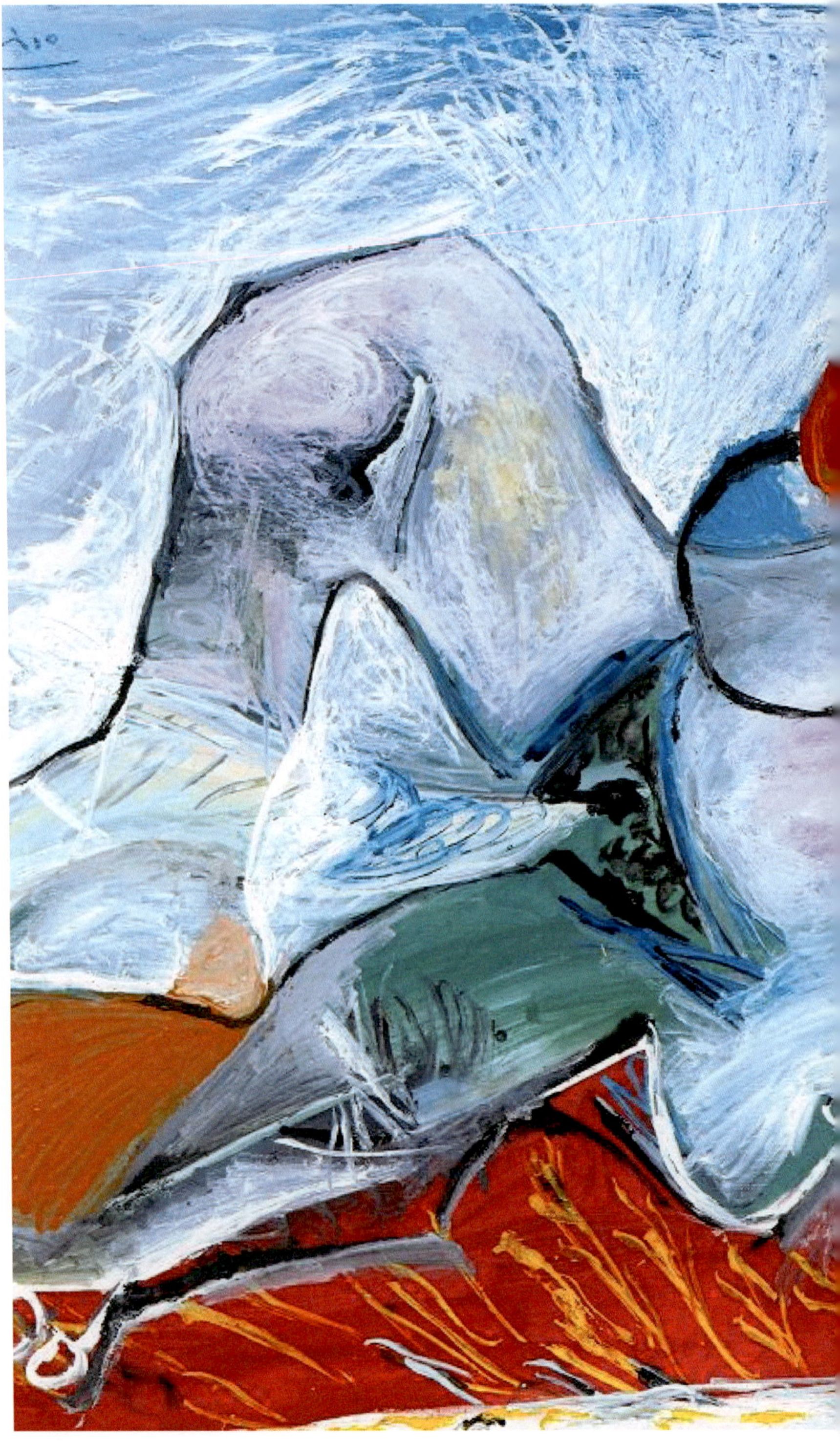

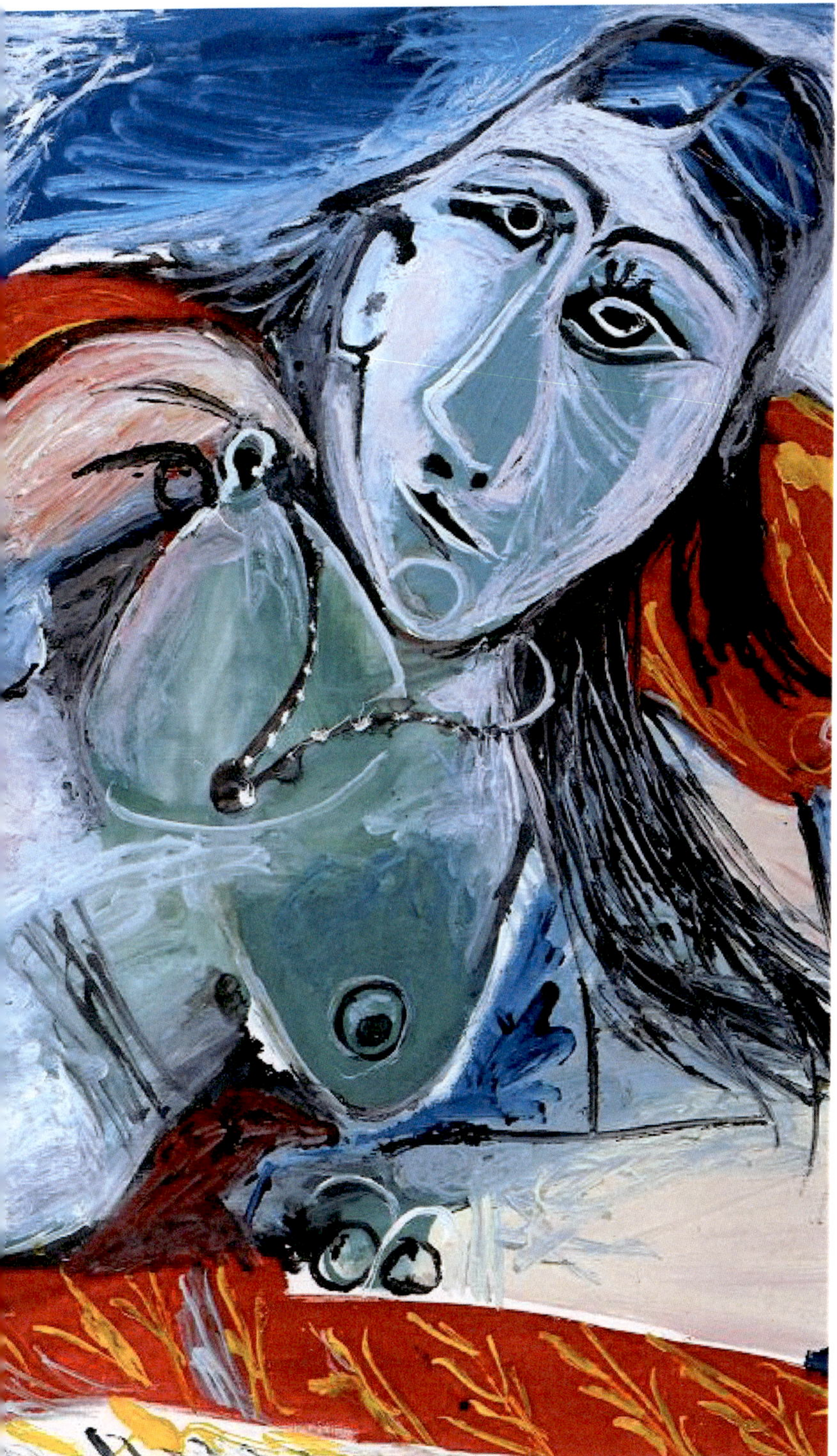

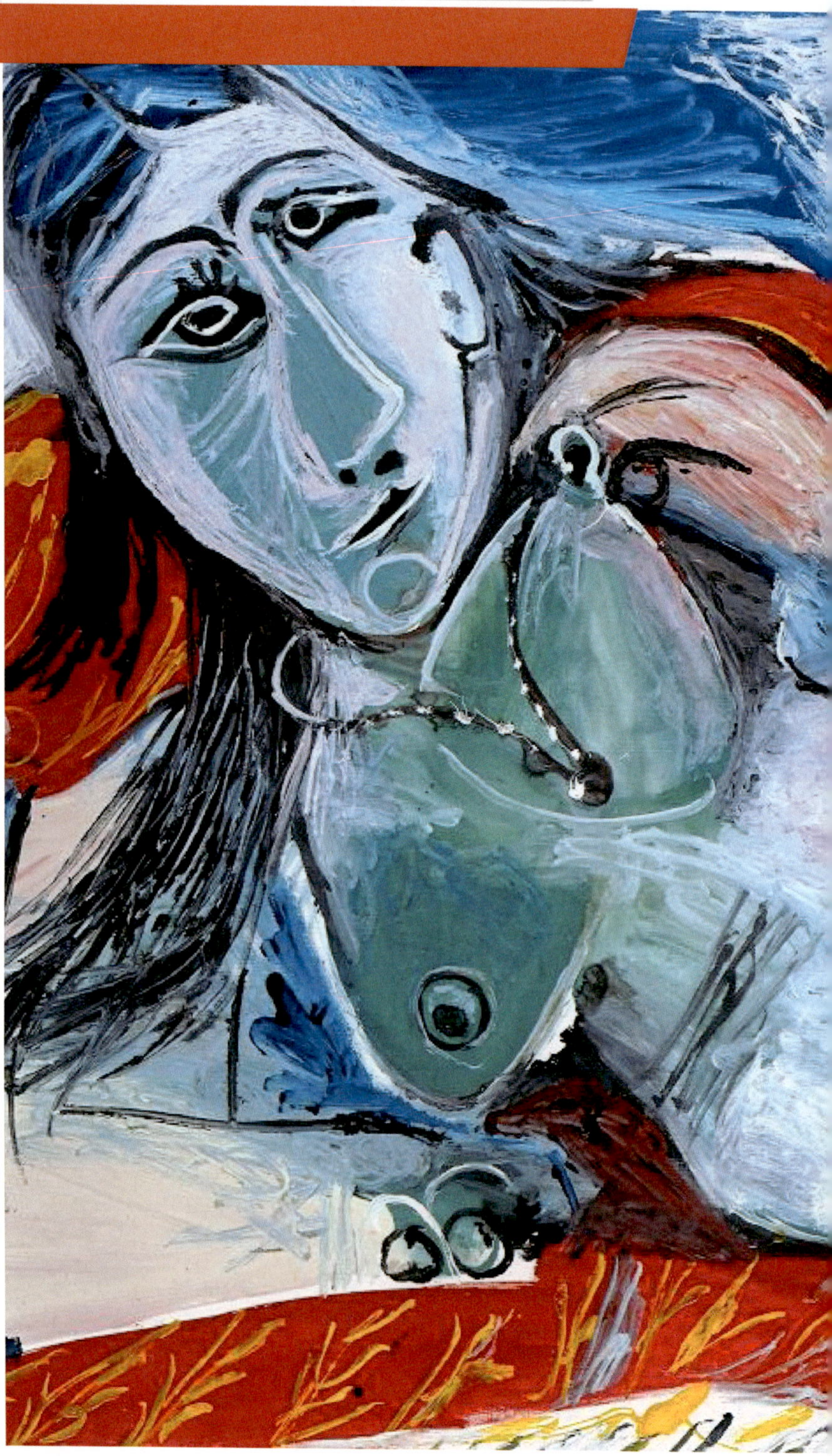

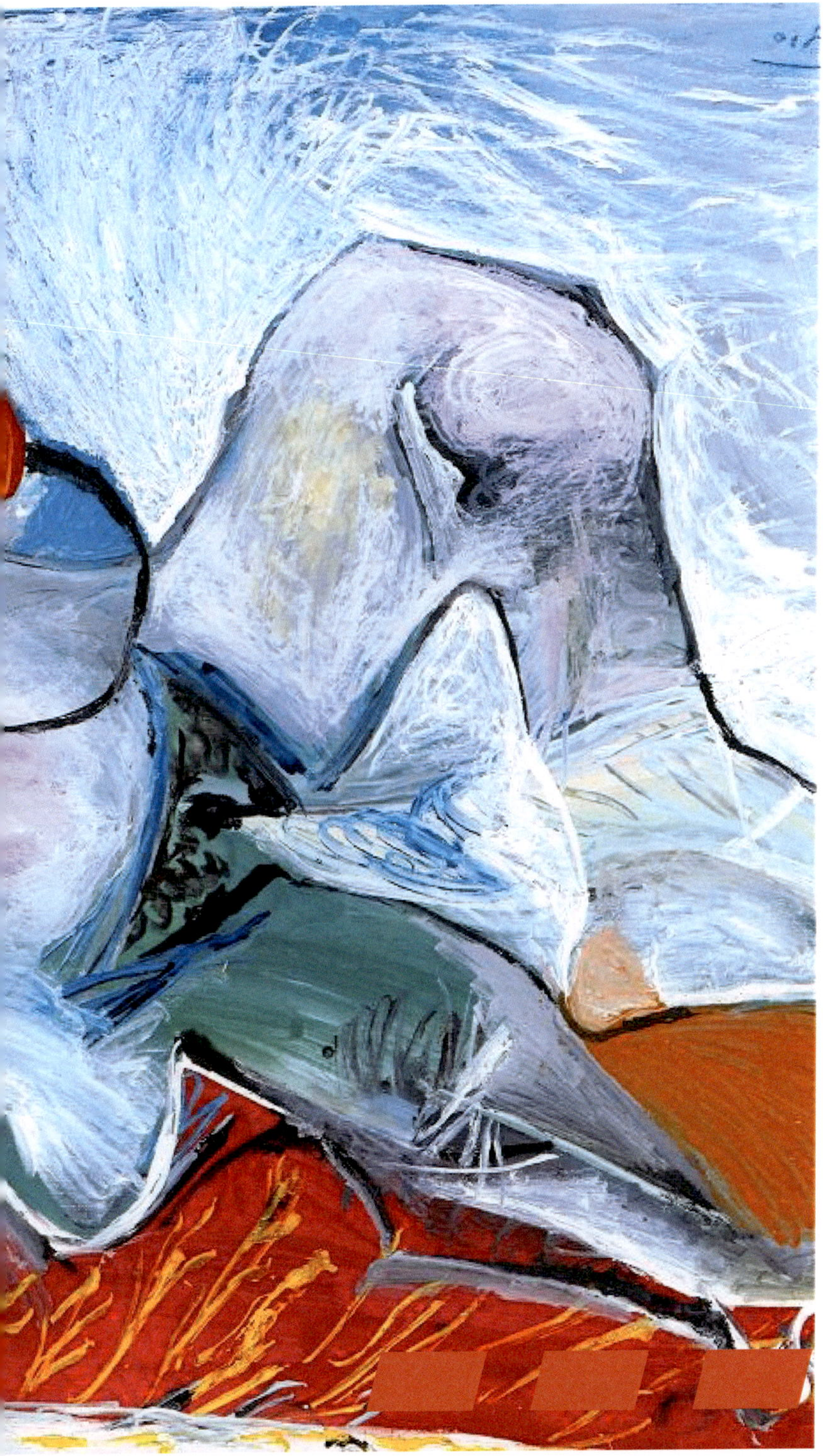

one for all the HOBB head$$£$...

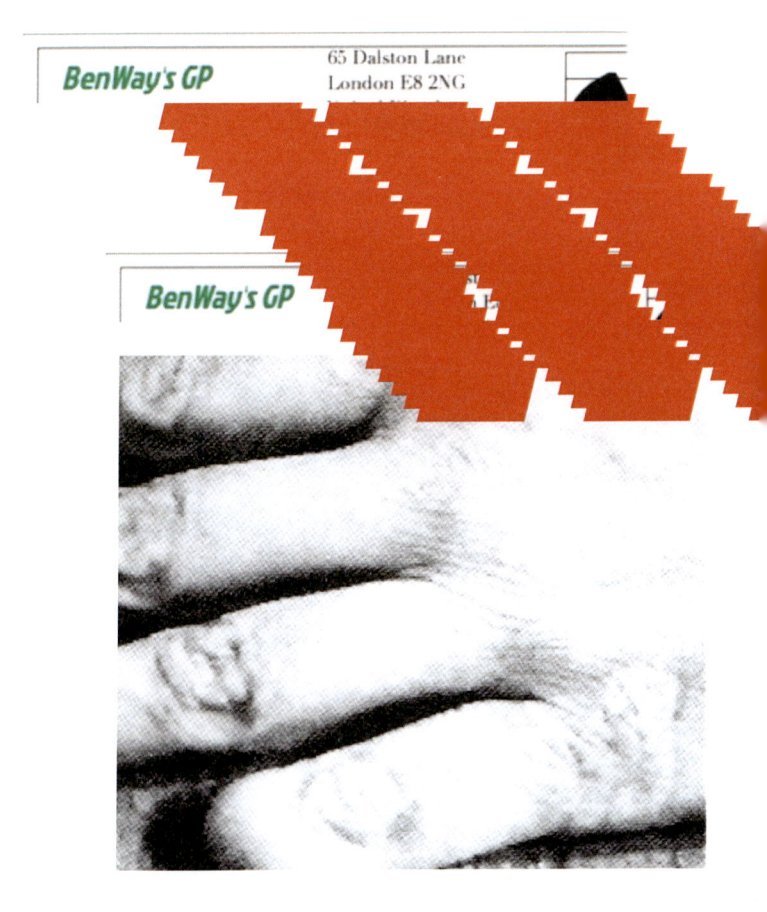

BenWay's GP 65 Dalston Lane
London E8 2NG

BenWay's GP

ROMANIAN HANDS OVER THE LOVE (
$$$$$$$$$$$$$$SAVEMESOCATF
YOUOOIOOOOOOO......

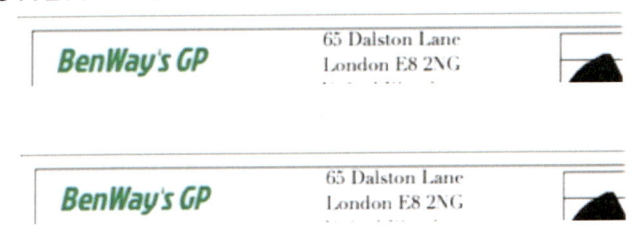

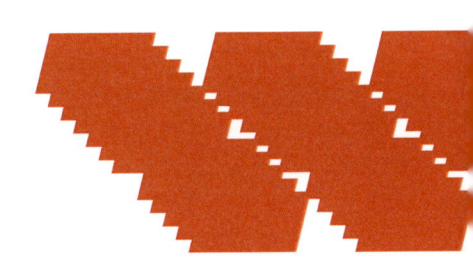

BenWay's GP
65 Dalston Lane
London E8 2NG

OOOIIIIIIIIIIIOOOOOOOOFFFFOOOOIIIIIIIIDDDDDDDDDDISSSSSS
VENTYONEANDSENDNIETSZCHEGODAWAYFROMT

BenWay's GP
65 Dalston Lane
London E8 2NG

BenWay's GP
65 Dalston Lane
London E8 2NG

84

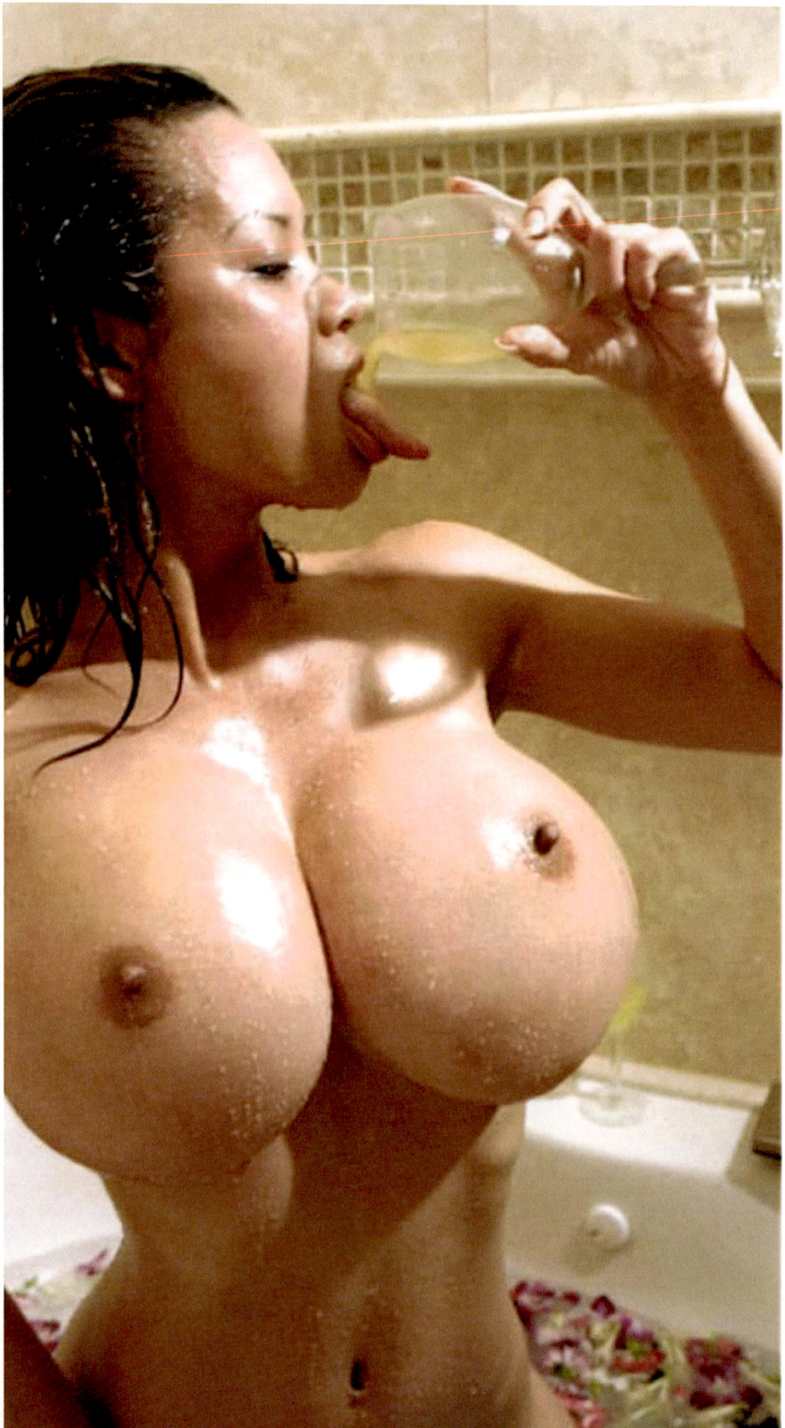

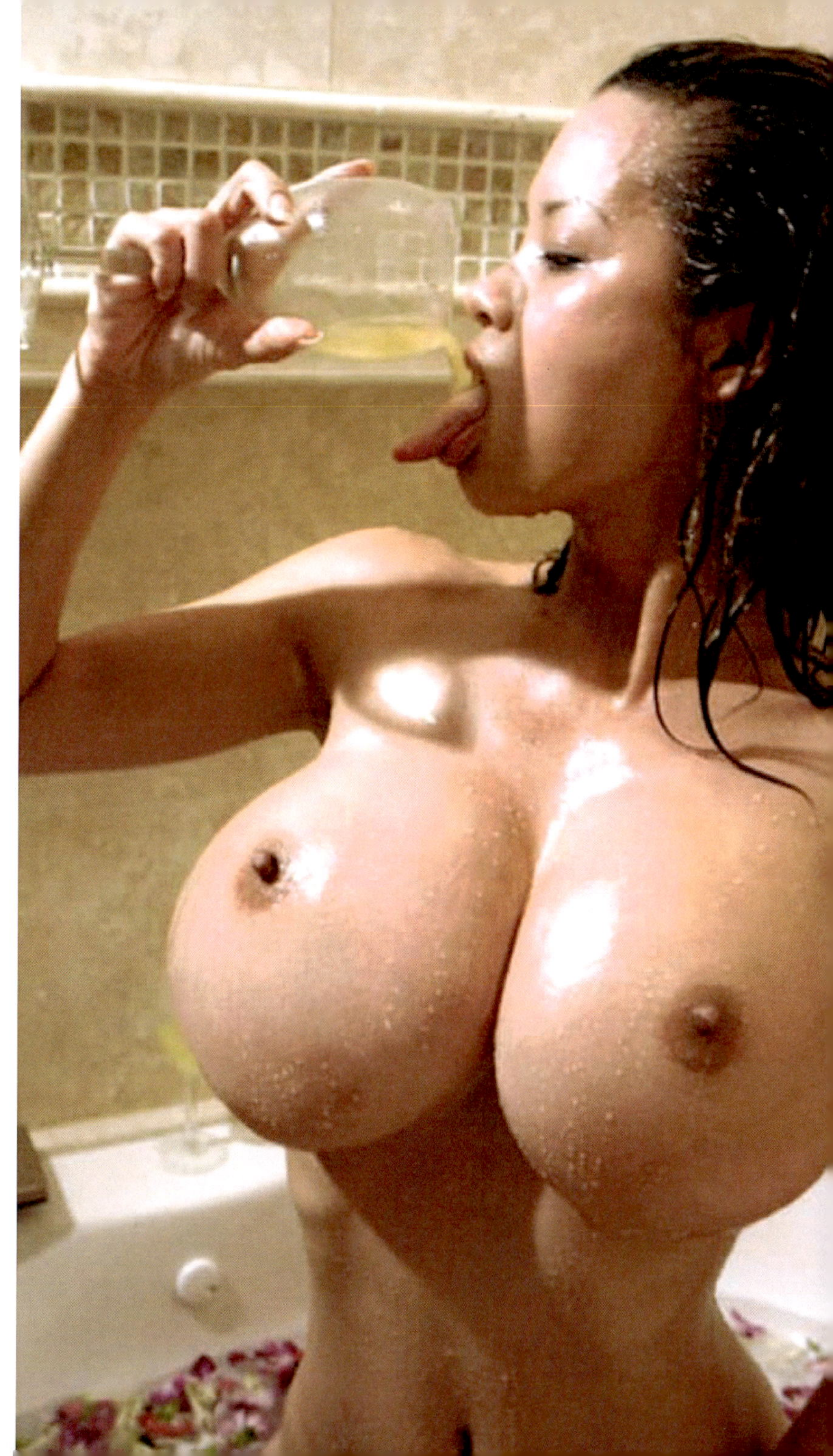

BenWay's GP 65 Dalston Lane London E8 2NG

...so what he said is...'GONNA DO MASELF OVA' IN THE WEE HOUR$$$...

...thán go ahead...with the FUEGO & the QUICKNESS...as, if you don't LOVE it here & i mean this as í don't either...then just take this PRESCRIPTION...& BE GOOD......
...LITTLE JUNKY...
...LOVE HOARDER...

...JALOUSE GREEN EYED !!!
28 x Medical Marijuana
28 x Lemsip...
2 x E45 (FOR BIG FOOT PROBLEM...
...)

COCOA BUTTER KISSES...

BenWay's GP   65 Dalston Lane
London E8 2NG

their problem...with no COCOA &/or
QUICKNESS...or, if you can't LOVE them & i mean
means i can't either...then just take this
PRESCRIPTION...& BE GOOD...
...LITTLE JUNKY...
...LOVE HOARDER...

...JALOUSE GREEN EYED !!!

28 x Medinal Marijuana
28 x Lemon...
the messy prescriptions$$$ *FOR BIG FOOT PROBLEM...*
the messy prescriptions$$$
the messy prescriptions$$$...

88

llOllD

BenWay's GP   65 Dalston Lane
London E8 2NG

...due to á worry as the next aution of the 'big white period Panties' she think's will happen tonigjt 'tonight tonight' she says...advise to take things easy...sleep early...go for a walk...when your husband's not looking perhaps take CHANCIE for a walk...come back whenever you Love...

4 x Lemsip
just half a bottle of Shampoo
a drip of eye dropS...yuuummmy...her eyes...deep dark against her soft skin & pixie haír with vaseline lips...

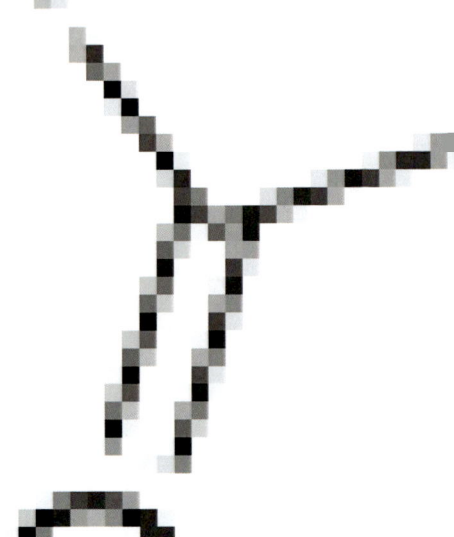

65 Dalston Lane
London E8 2NG

BenWay's GP

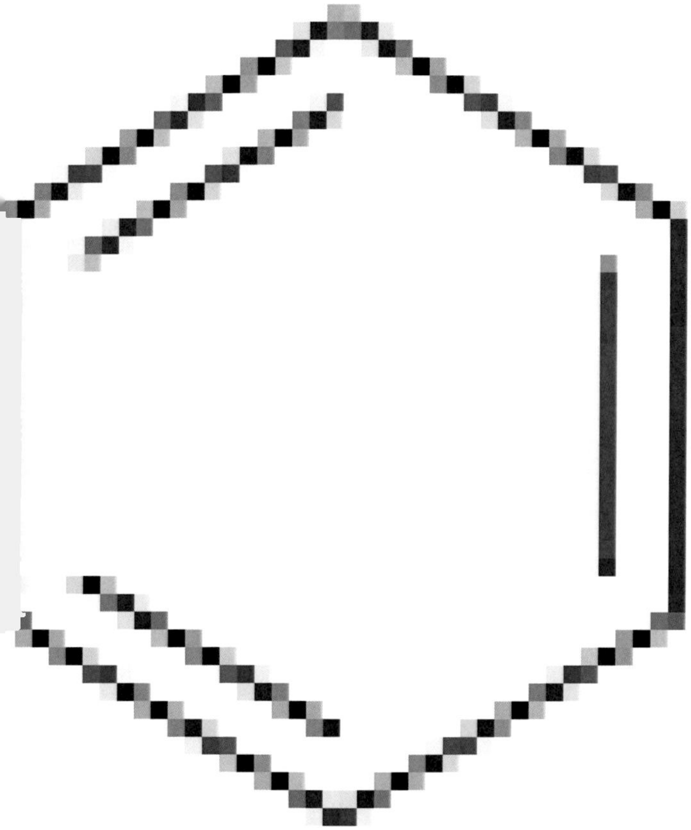

BenWay's GP   65 Dalston Lane
London E8 2NG

...memo to self...let's just go to her house...oh no no..that would break the Hippottomus Oath on this here wall...Ishmael & our 'MUMBO JUMBO' pack would not stand for this nonsense...í can't let her know í stalk her like Celina...she will only not cum...& i want her to cum cum cum cum cum cum cum...all on this MAN IN THE MIRROR...

BenWay's GP   65 Dalston Lane
London E8 2NG

malotov..!

maybe perhaps if so can be ya know?

DASH a KADDISH LIKE SO MAYER...

BenWay's GP 65 Dalston Lane
London E8 2NG

Y

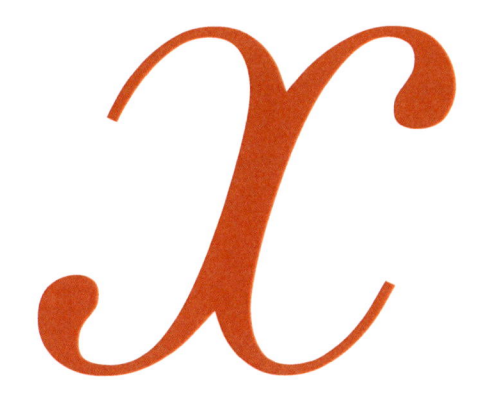

BenWay's GP 65 Dalston Lane
London E8 2NG

x

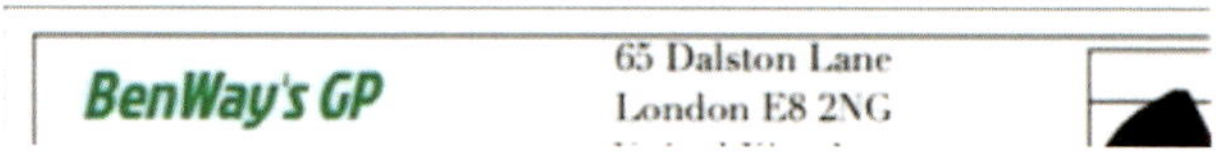

BenWay's GP

65 Dalston Lane
London E8 2NG

BenWay's GP 65 Dalston Lane
London E8 2NG

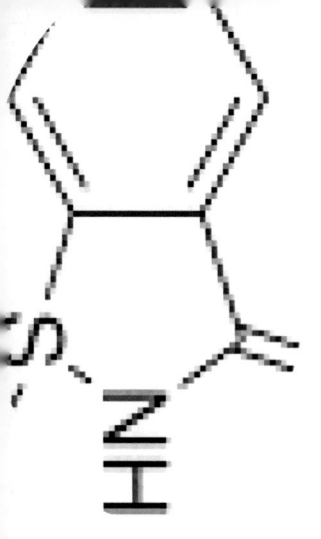

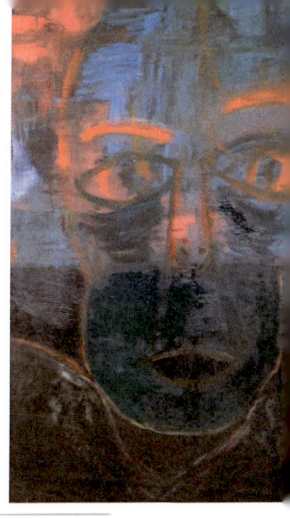

...grumbling about takin' his 'bawl & chain' & the rest...take this Soup...

E45 (Dave's Brand for Xtra Crispy Skeen$)

BenWay's GP　　　65 Dalston Lane
　　　　　　　　　　London E8 2NG

...what a long summer it's been...it's (chunky monkey) apparently & so it goes...as HER HUSBAND IS NO MORE HER$... cheerio...good day to listen to the Beautiful noise...

...as it's September 'Reign' now...as she says...it's her hundred & fourty fourth time that this de ja vuing DREAM i$ troublin' ma $OUI...that this DREAM's occurred... GYNCOLOGI$T !!!

GOD SAVE MA SOUL

'i'm about to bleeaooouuueeefff' off apparently (she was adamant about her use of the 'chubbyback' word 'bleeaooouuueeefff'...

BenWay's GP 65 Dalston Lane
London E8 2NG

...talkin' of 'Fin$' & being a total 'messup' & that she's in some sort of 'passa' as she has scratch marks all over her labia......as if arriving like a fish too an inn...'LIKE a hotel for fi$H' & that 'she's drowning in the waters as she's so wet' due to some 'MARCUS or TYRONE'...more waters.& 'needin' to pee' í'm advising SHE go to the Loouurvé or the LOO as she then sceams...'Nuuuuts!' with the taste of RED WíNE all over even now...I am faded & can smell the RED WíNE...ooo..her Pussy or (Iabia) moistens...

56 x Lemsip
10 x Vitamin D...

BenWay's GP

65 Dalston Lane
London E8 2NG

BenWay's GP 65 Dalston Lane
London E8 2NG

DESCARTIAN LAW$...

BenWay's GP   65 Dalston Lane
London E8 2NG

BenWay's GP 65 Dalston Lane
London E8 2NG

...the summer's been so long...since the last appointment...all I've got at home is the 'administrator' to keep me ventilated (HEII IT'$ HOT AS DANTE WITH TITS OUT)...the ocean doesn't need anymore of these here tears...

FLU Jab
Castor Oil
turboclous Jabs (as TlME with this 'Holly' who is 'apparently his mistress' is suggested)

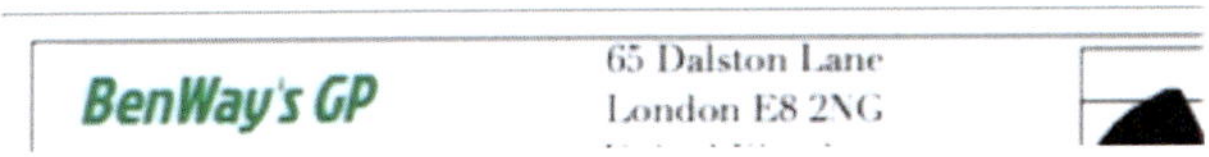

BenWay's GP

65 Dalston Lane
London E8 2NG

BenWay's GP 65 Dalston Lane
London E8 2NG

                                                              she dropped the ff$TEW
                                                                                        ff$TEW...
                                                                                   ...ffSTEW...
                                                                                  ffSTEW...
                                                                               ...ffSTEW

she dropped the ff$TEW   ...ffSTEW...ffSTEW...
ff$TEW...
...ffSTEW...
ffSTEW...
...ff$TEW
...ff$TEW...ff$TEW...

a futurist...poem 'inconcieved' of
Tristan Tzarza...

        prescribe an Almodovár Motion
        Pain Ting...

                                                              gff$TEW...don't
                                                               stew...

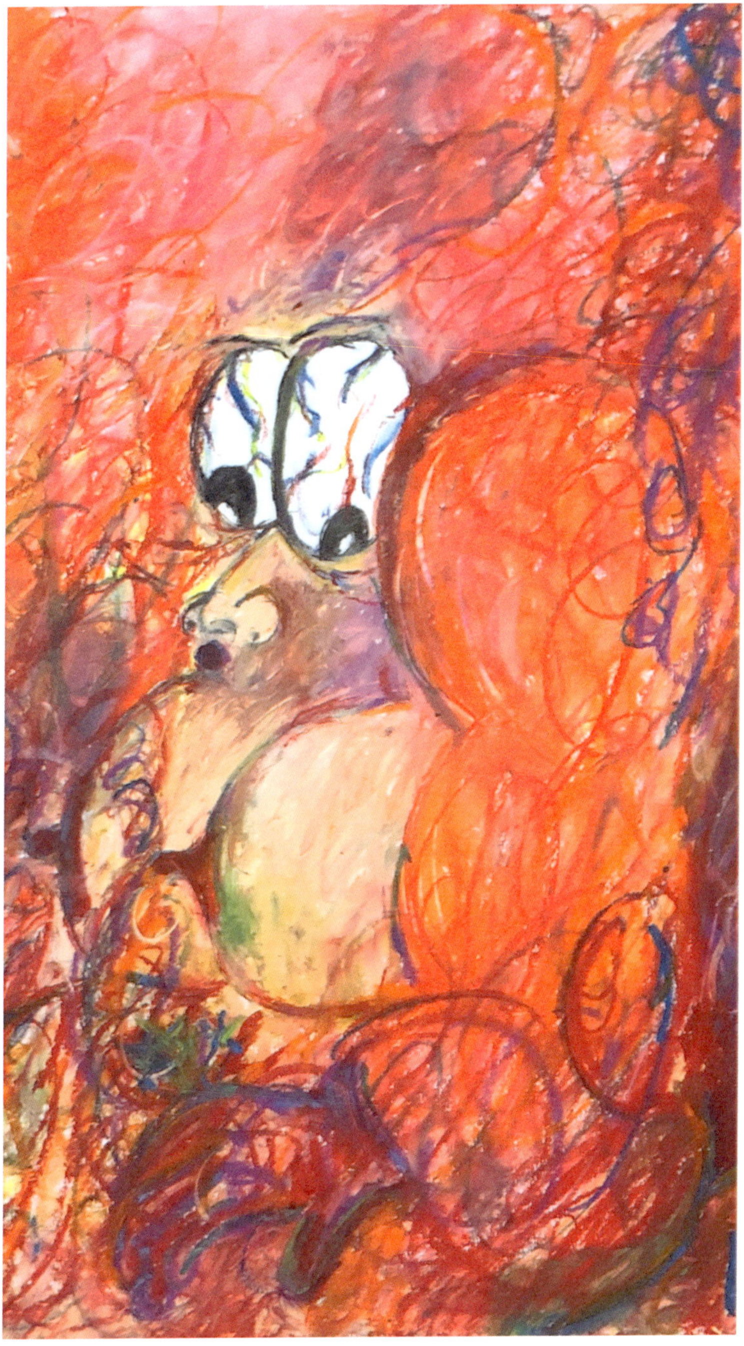

he

Y

BenWay's GP 65 Dalston Lane
London E8 2NG

BenWay's GP 65 Dalston Lane
London E8 2NG

...what a long summer...cheerio it's September 'Reign' as she says...it's her hundred & fourty fourth time this DREAM's occurred...GYNCOLOGI$T !!! 'i'm about to bleeaooouuueeefff' off apparently (she was adamant about her use of the 'chubbyback' word 'bleeaooouuueeefff'...

Try Another Brand of Shampoos
20 x Rosewater
Staccoto Sumpsions...
7x Lempsíp...

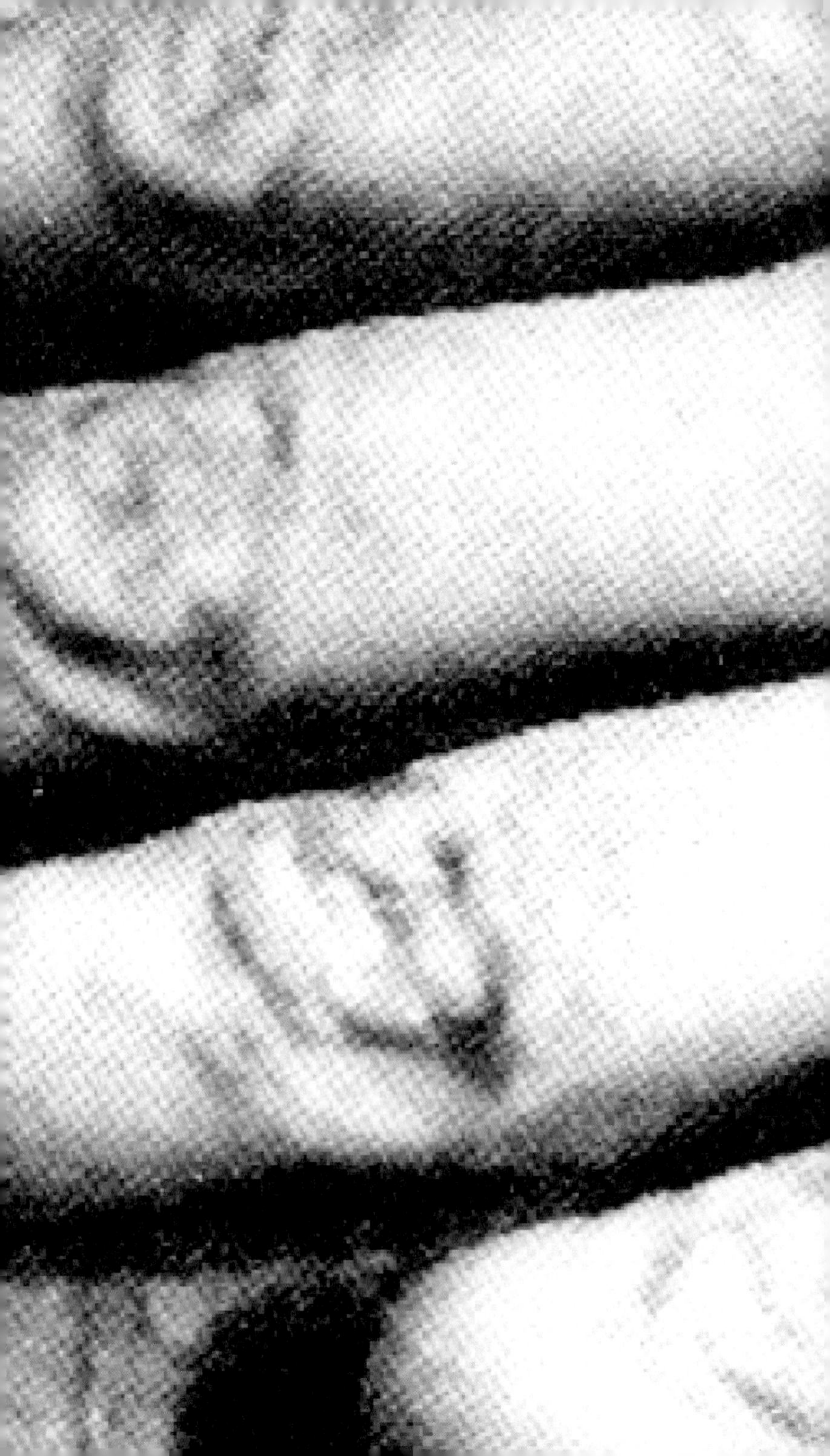

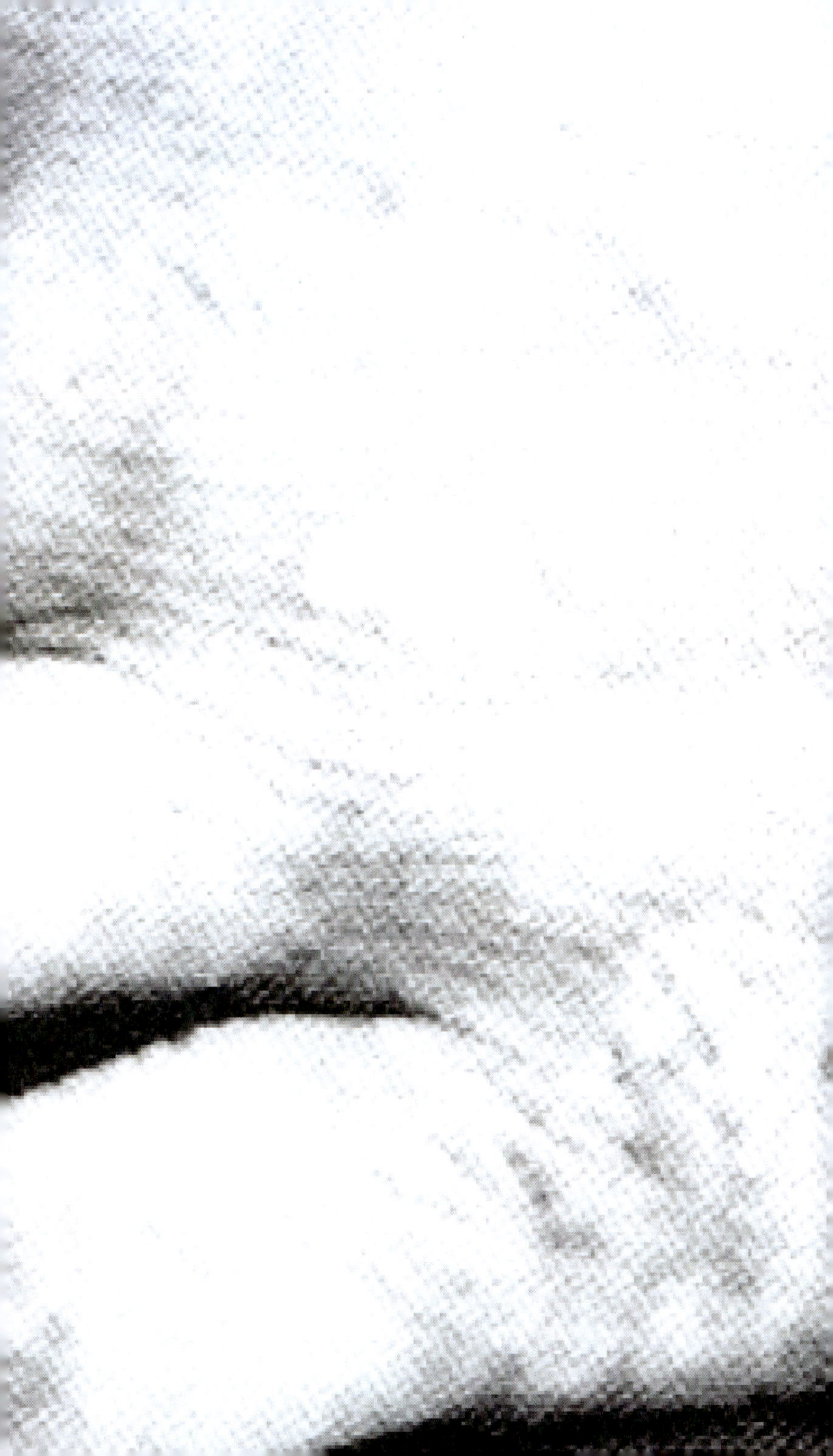

\OI' GP HISTORY

nineteen eighty four

BenWay's GP 65 Dalston Lane
London E8 2NG

...always with Vinní & getting Hair &
Scalp...Prescribe...

meningiTITS Gab*
sleep early
for all the bed wetting & mílk drinking from
Roth's Mother's Titty...*that's your Mother's !!!

...obsessed with sweets...cavities in four a
cannínes..
*knowwonder *Celeste Bullies this Kid...*

*notes on this twat

Mr Marcus

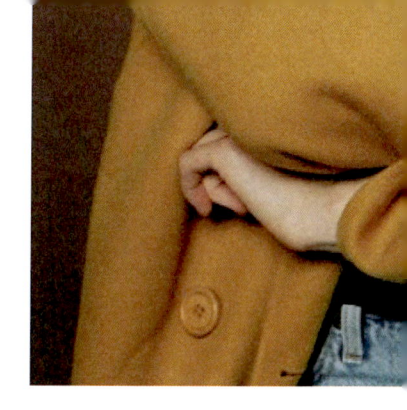

BenWay's GP 65 Dalston Lane
London E8 2NG

BenWay's GP 65 Dalston Lane
London E8 2NG

..FLU JAB...

¿

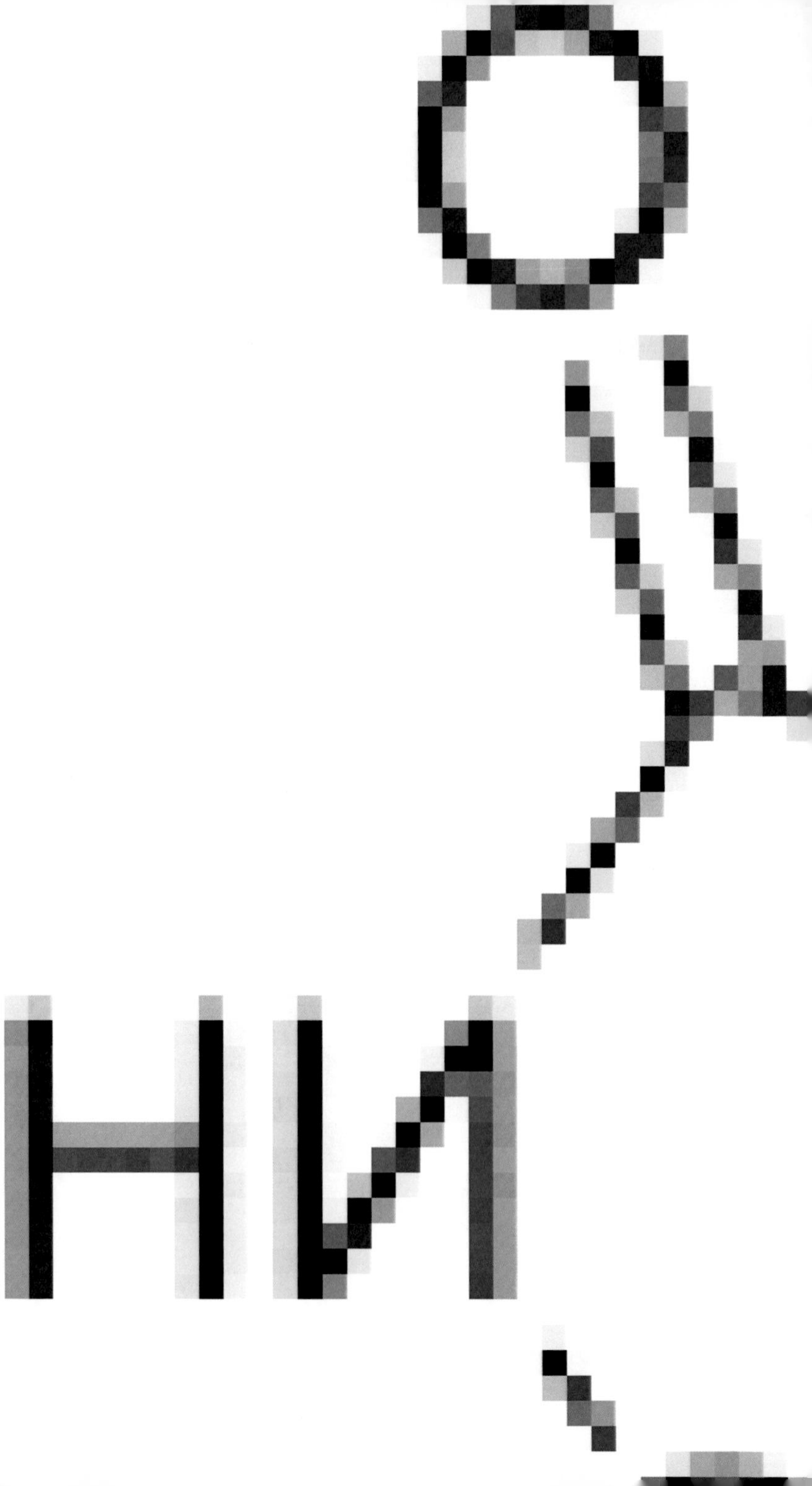
O
HN

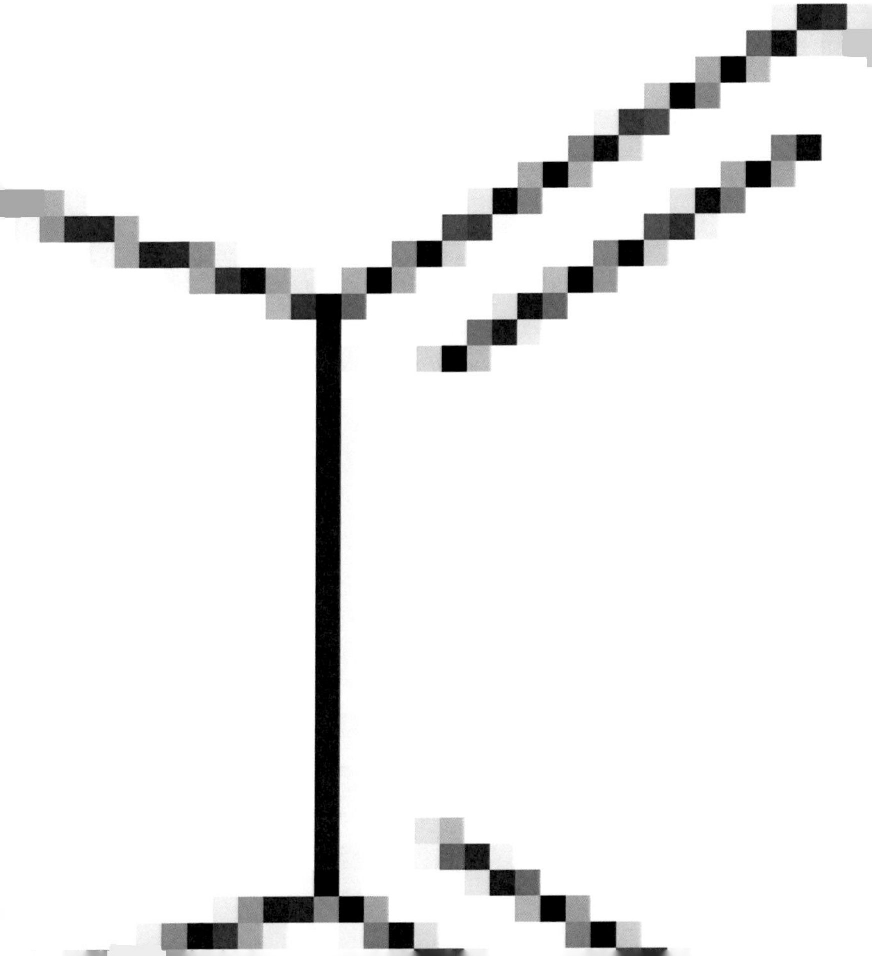

HE
HAN

BOBTHOMPSONXVIVIANBROWNJMBXKB...COPYRIGHT...

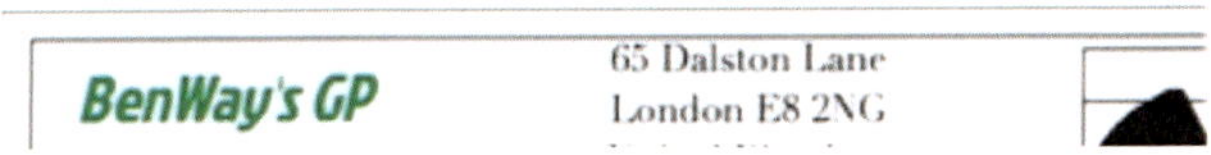

BenWay's GP

65 Dalston Lane
London E8 2NG

...APPARENTLY SHE IS
WATCHING...

LOVE I$LAND
$EX & THE CITY
TOWIE
$OPRANO$
GOMORRAH

BenWay's GP 65 Dalston Lane
London E8 2NG

GYNO IV

CÕOK RICE...
OR LEARN
& DON'T BURN THE STEW !!!

...

Dr. Danadoní

place of Birth & currently residing in residency in Daubeney, Hackney after time, like Edward Burra...

BenWay's GP 65 Dalston Lane
London E8 2NG

GYNO SIX

BenWay's GP 65 Dalston Lane
London E8 2NG

...Tuberculous Jab required...GIVEN, as she needs to get away & not get Painted Over by Thi$ God that i$ not hear to listen...listen...listen...(GYNO appointment two Months in advance...so cum...back safe & maybe DIVORCE) as she says......í can't take this farcial marriage anymore...though...appafrently it's legal binding marks that scratch...this PUNK Marriage...know what what what !!!!...(stuttering in Pain TíNG) so prescribing a STRONG DOSE OF VITAMIN D...

X

...í'm glad í'm now now now...heading to Varanasi as I need to see the Uncle Geoff & Alain's Mago Tree$...she says...

x 50 Cod Liver Oil...

RlKKl'$ CAT

..

a haiku learnt from ONE Hiro (go quicker not sumimasen!!!)

BenWay's GP 65 Dalston Lane
London E8 2NG

(GYNO appointment two Months from NOW) as she says......í can't take this farcial marriage with you know who who who...(stuttering in Pain) í'm glad í'm heading to Varanasi as I need to see the Uncle Geoff)

BenWay's GP　　65 Dalston Lane
　　　　　　　　　London E8 2NG

...'oooouuueeefff' arriving & mentionig it going off at 'work' & as a MAN we all require work...please take this PRESCRIPTION & break a leg...

99x Lemsip
Medical Marijuana
14 x Pepto Bismal (& come back in two months...but but but Adorno...says take in equal measure to giving...so take this three times a day & *...)

BenWay's GP 65 Dalston Lane
London E8 2NG

PicaSSO's BIG BALLS

quoted from La D Davignon at Mougins...

BenWay's GP 65 Dalston Lane
London E8 2NG

BenWay's GP

65 Dalston Lane
London E8 2NG

BenWay's GP

65 Dalston Lane
London E8 2NG

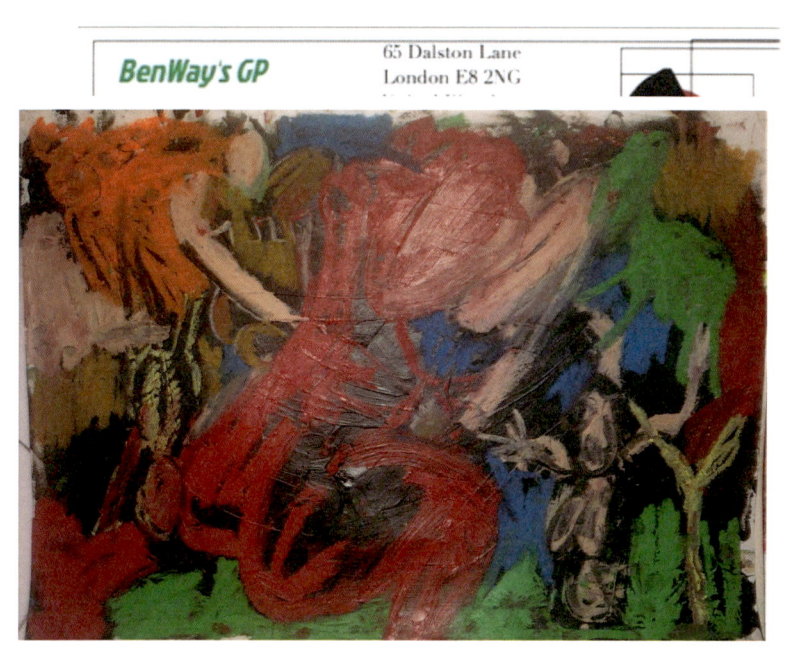

...so so so GOOD... sessions where you called this one shooting PLATO of your DREAM...

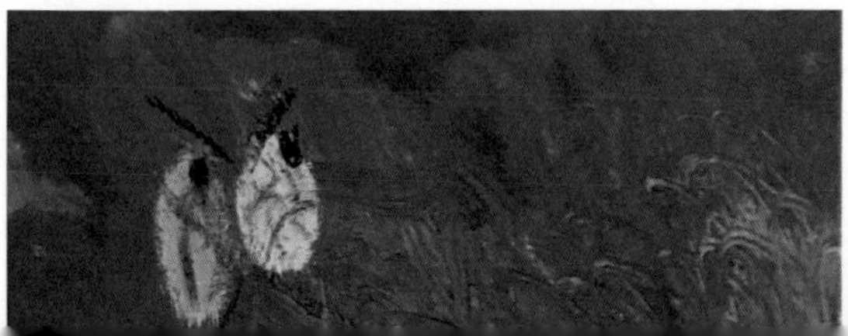

BenWay's GP 65 Dalston Lane London E8 2NG

(....*) redacted in a COURT of LAW CLINTON STYLE moreso due to a 'Young Thug' ODin'...ha$$$!!! of the LAW !!! ha$$$$!!!? i prescribed an Easter Terry's Chocolate Orange I saíd..! í advise not harming Kat neither...KAT'$ KITTY IS MINE!!!!

28 x Lempsip...
ffs x 99p

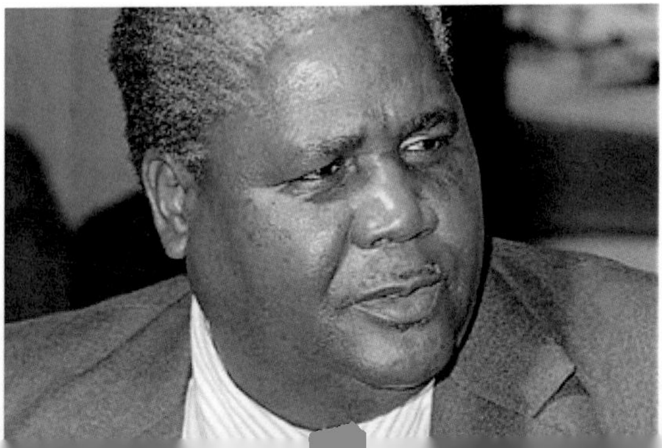

BenWay's GP 65 Dalston Lane
London E8 2NG

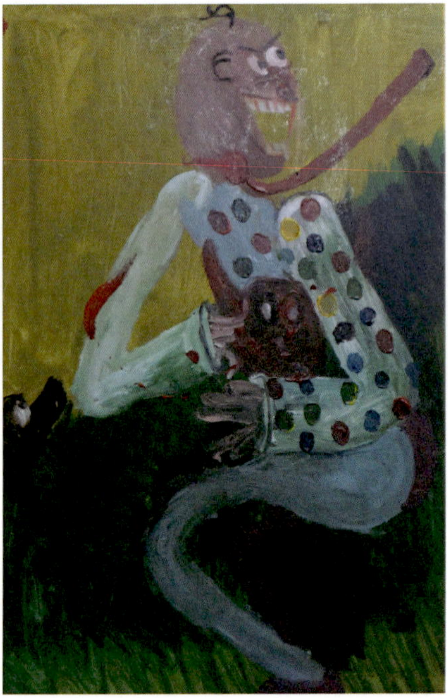

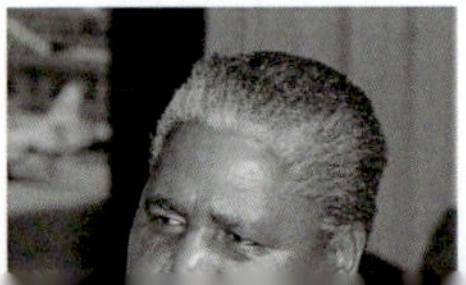

BenWay's GP

65 Dalston Lane
London E8 2NG

BenWay's GP

65 Dalston Lane
London E8 2NG

BenWay's GP

65 Dalston Lane
London E8 2NG

BenWay's GP 65 Dalston Lane
London E8 2NG

BenWay's GP 65 Dalston Lane
London E8 2NG

BenWay's GP 65 Dalston Lane
London E8 2NG

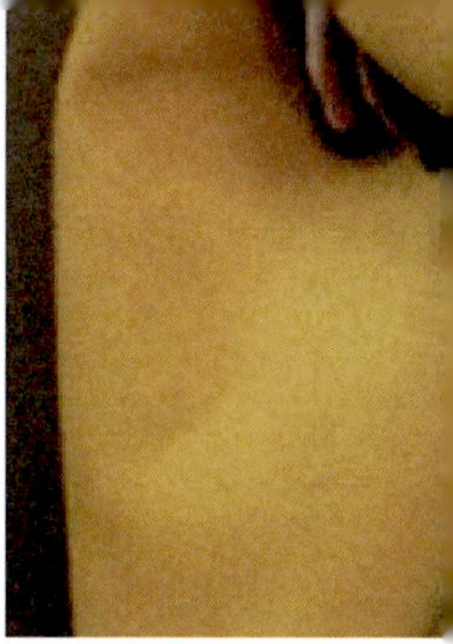

...ÍS THE SUN LOOKIN' WHEN I'M NOT STARRING LIKE LYNCH DOES IN HER 'DREAMS' SHE NOW CALLS...

BenWay's GP   65 Dalston Lane
               London E8 2NG

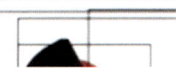

ERA$ER

DRIPS

NON
MEEDI...

BenWay's GP   65 Dalston Lane
London E8 2NG

...all í seem to have is TIME...she mentions this...as something í ought to Prescribe for...mentioning a friend in 'DREAMS' named Ann Quinn, who watches 'MEMENTO'..ok gorgeous...*

....*

[
yx

redacted]...advise a daily Gynecologi$t appointment...just take the PRESCRIPTION from EIIE for the Bellyache problems...

BenWay's GP 65 Dalston Lane
London E8 2NG

...all í seem to have is TIME...she mentions this...*

....*

redacted...advise a daily Gynecologi$t appointment...just take the PRESCRIPTION from EllE for the GUT's problems...

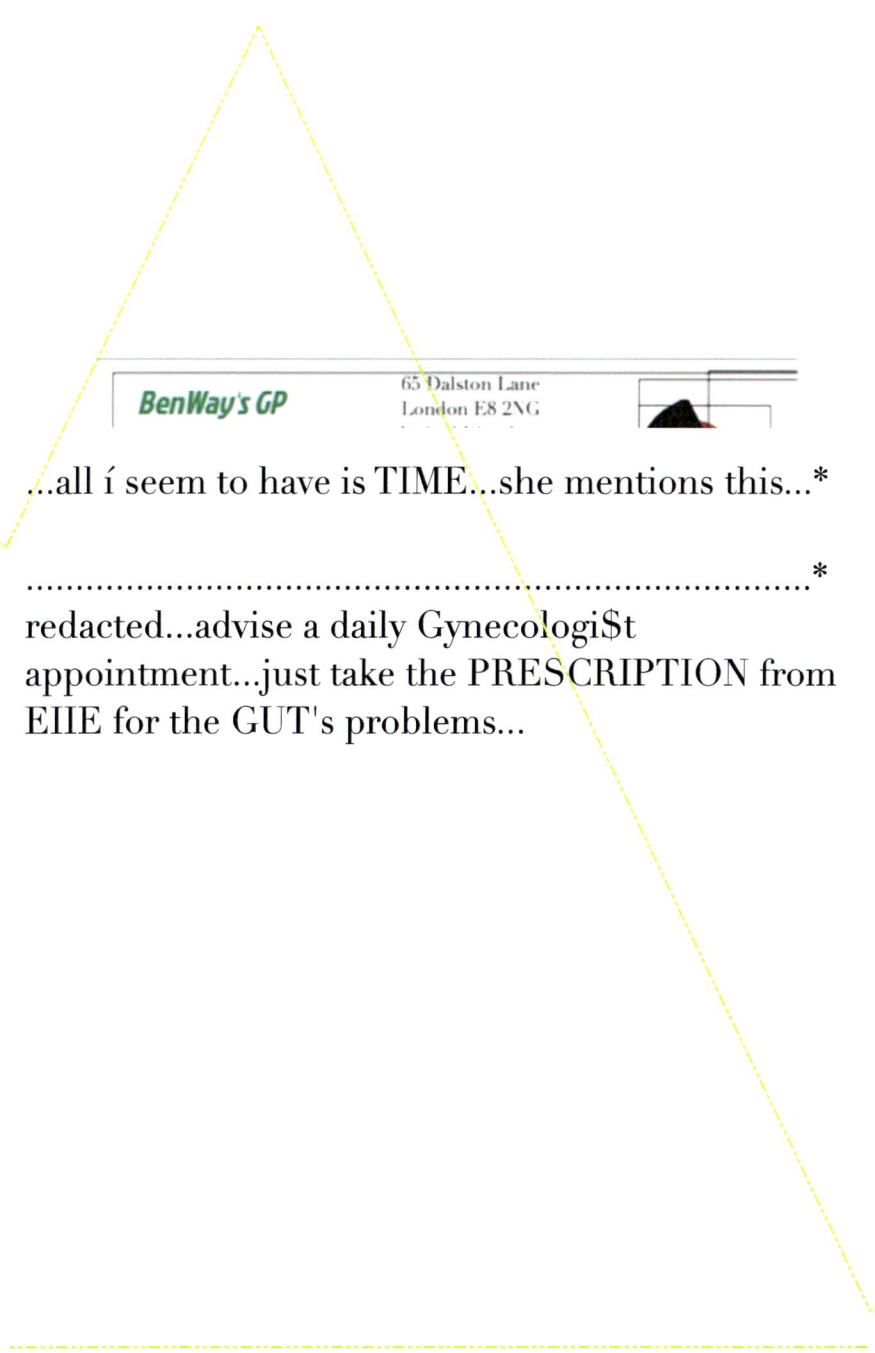

Guinness DAYS

Olá...

Olá Olá

BenWay's GP 65 Dalston Lane
London E8 2NG

...ooooooooeeefff...beside thís
PRESCRIPTION precipitating your ability
to be...to be beautiful...to be a gorgeous
lemon (god? wash a lemon will ya') just
take theé walks...
Staccato Cumsíon$
Lemsip
Pepto
BismooooooooooooooooooooooooooooooooooooooooOOOOOOOOOOOOaaaaaaaaa
aaaaaaaaaamaH...why...
...í'll be at the FUNERAL of your
HUSBAND..! ....and want to know HOW HE
DIED ooo !
...priaprism...

Olá

BenWay's GP   65 Dalston Lane
London E8 2NG

…with a summer's day with0ut *theé í*…more more more Lemsip's $ípping in the lungs of this here heart's desire…Jue out 'ere Bindlestiffing the deathly Prescriptions wrong one…perhaps Lady.Day…it was Prescribe…You Had Me at HELLO AKWABA
Ola *Lady.Dáy…*

PRIAPRISM

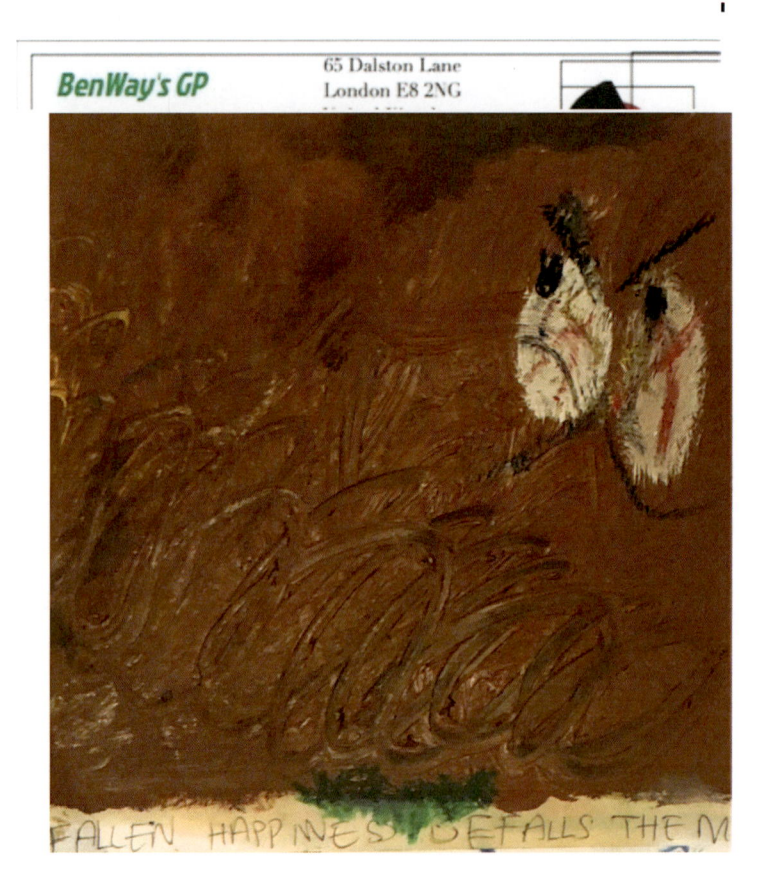

BenWay's GP 65 Dalston Lane
London E8 2NG

FALLEN HAPPINESS BEFALLS THE M

!

BenWay's GP 65 Dalston Lane
London E8 2NG

!

RSUS...

IIOIID

Pablo Picasso...
Nude Womam with Pearl Necklace
oil on canvas
113.5 x 116.7 cm
1968

[taken at TATE MODERN 2015 which was first purchased, 1986]

other bits & peaces...

pages...eighty too...eighty five fíve...contains a collage consisting of artworks;
@KEHN
@waynex
Urda Heidi Aloösa...
@KofiPaints
Corona Y.....
Homerton UT...
L.J...
Dean Blunt's 'Brutal' inspired page 90 too...

front cover interpolates calligraphy& collage by Urda Heidi Aloösa...
Existential Tithead
Oil, acrylic & oil pastel on board
30 x 40 cm
2023
[in a private collection]

special congrats to the Black God íN The NIGHT SKY...

...a few other works...

...lo fi dreams...

...mango...

...fuego...

...fuego IV

...fiesta of charms...

...lady. day...

...juice (limited iTalian edition)

...couple poems & that...(2009)

...fuego trilogy (III)

..Mr. Fantastic (previously Published... OpenPen...

Vanity.Ares

next...2040...stripped down woop woop essays on laughphobia...

BenWay's GP

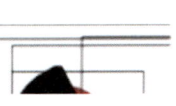

65 Dalston Lane
London E8 2NG

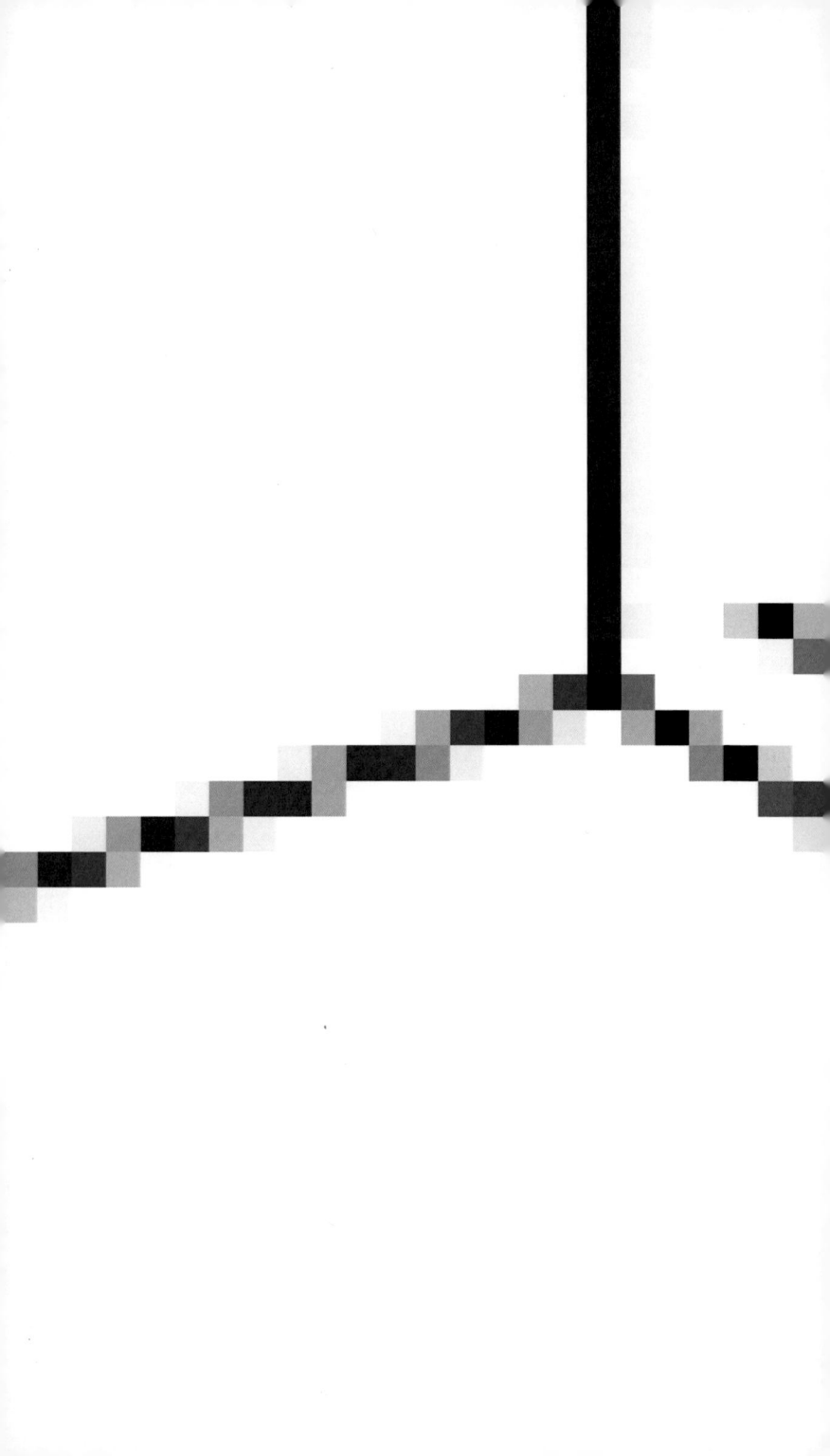

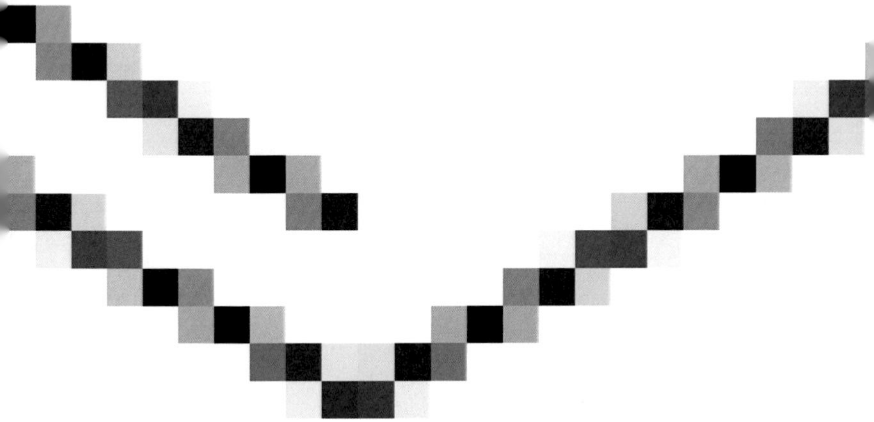

Milton Keynes UK
Ingram Content Group UK Ltd.
UKRC030753230424
441594UK00005B/109